Adventures in JapaNese 1

アドベンチャー日本語

Workbook
with Hiragana/Katakana and Kanji

4TH EDITION

Hiromi Peterson & Naomi Hirano-Omizo

Junko Ady & Jan Asato

Illustrated by Michael Muronaka

CHENG & TSUI COMPANY

Boston

3rd Printing   2018
20 19 18   3 4 5 6 7 8 9 10 11

Published by
Cheng & Tsui Company
25 West Street
Boston, MA 02111-1213 USA
Phone (617) 988-2400 / (800) 554-1963
Fax (617) 426-3669
chengtsui.co
"Bringing Asia to the World" ™

Adventures in Japanese Vol. 1 Workbook, 4th Edition:
ISBN: 978-1-62291-057-1

The *Adventures in Japanese* series includes textbooks, workbooks, teacher guides, audio downloads, and a companion website at **chengtsui.co/adventuresinjapanese**.

Visit **chengtsui.co** for more information on *Adventures in Japanese* and additional Japanese language resources.

Printed in the United States of America

TABLE OF
Contents

Hiragana

	W	R	Y	M	H	N	T	S	K		
ん (n)	わ	ら	や	ま	は	な	た	さ	か	あ	A
		り		み	ひ	に	ち (chi)	し (shi)	き	い	I
		る	ゆ	む	ふ	ぬ	つ (tsu)	す	く	う	U
		れ		め	へ	ね	て	せ	け	え	E
を (O)	ろ	よ	も	ほ	の	と	そ	こ	お	O

(Particle)

P	B	
ぱ	ば	A
ぴ	び	I
ぷ	ぶ	U
ぺ	べ	E
ぽ	ぼ	O

D	Z	G	
だ	ざ	が	A
ぢ (ji)	じ (ji)	ぎ	I
づ (zu)	ず (zu)	ぐ	U
で	ぜ	げ	E
ど	ぞ	ご	O

Katakana

W		R	Y	M	H	N	T	S	K	
ン n	ワ	ラ	ヤ	マ	ハ	ナ	タ	サ	カ	ア A
		リ		ミ	ヒ	ニ	チ chi	シ shi	キ	イ I
		ル	ユ	ム	フ	ヌ	ツ tsu	ス	ク	ウ U
		レ		メ	ヘ	ネ	テ	セ	ケ	エ E
	ヲ O	ロ	ヨ	モ	ホ	ノ	ト	ソ	コ	オ O

(Particle)

P	B
パ	バ
ピ	ビ
プ	ブ
ペ	ベ
ポ	ボ

D	Z	G	
ダ	ザ	ガ	A
ヂ ji	ジ ji	ギ	I
ヅ zu	ズ zu	グ	U
デ	ゼ	ゲ	E
ド	ゾ	ゴ	O

Kanji

Kanji with a + before them are new readings.

3か	一	二	三	四	五	日	名前	
	いち, ひと (つ)	に, ふた (つ)	さん, みっ (つ)	し, よ, よん, よっ (つ)	ご, いつ (つ)	に, にち, ひ, び, か	なまえ	
4か	六	七	八	九	十	月	明日	
	ろく, むっ (つ)	なな, しち, なな (つ)	はち, やっ (つ)	きゅう, く, ここの (つ)	じゅう, とお	がつ, げつ, つき	あした	
5か	火	水	木	金	土	本	曜	
	か, ひ	みず, すい	き, もく	かね, きん	ど, つち	もと, ほん, ぼん, ぽん	よう	
6か	口	目	耳	手	父	母	上手	下手
	くち, ぐち, こう	め, もく	みみ	て, しゅ	ちち, とう	はは, かあ	じょうず	へた

7か	分	行	来	車	山	川	時	
	わ (かります) ふん, ぷん, (ぶん)	い (きます), こう	き(ます)	くるま, しゃ	やま, さん	かわ, がわ	じ	
8か	人	子	女	好	田	男	私	
	ひと, にん, じん	こ	おんな	す (き)	た, だ	おとこ	わたし	
9か	先	生	今	毎	年	休	生徒	+来
	せん	せい	いま, こん	まい	とし, ねん	やす (み)	せいと	らい
10か	大	小	中	早	学	校	高校	
	おお (きい), だい	ちい (さい), しょう	ちゅう	はや (い)	がく, がっ	こう	こうこう	
11か	白	百	千	万	円	見	犬	太
	しろ (い)	ひゃく, びゃく, ぴゃく	せん, ぜん	まん	えん	み (る)	いぬ	ふと(る)
12か	天	牛	良	食	言	語	何	+一
	てん	ぎゅう	よ (い)	た(べる), しょく	い (う)	ご	なに, なん	いっ

なまえ *Namae* (Name) _____

ひづけ *Hizuke* (Date) _____ _____ ようび *Yoobi*
(Day of the week)

You may not know all the Japanese you hear, but use what you do know along with your imagination!

A **You will listen once to a series of conversations. Each question below refers to a different conversation. Choose the most appropriate answer to each question.**

1. What is Ken's telephone number?
   a. 674–2817
   b. 613–2817
   c. 673–2517
   d. 673–2817

2. What is Emi's telephone number?
   a. 923–8016
   b. 924–8016
   c. 923–8019
   d. 925–8016

3. What is the teacher's telephone number?
   a. 784–2691
   b. 734–2691
   c. 734–2091
   d. 734–2697

4. What is the school's telephone number?
   a. 944–8720
   b. 954–8720
   c. 944–6720
   d. 944–8730

B **You will listen once to a series of conversations. Each question below refers to a different conversation. Choose the most appropriate answer to each question.**

1. What situation best describes the conversation between the two speakers?
   a. A teacher and student greet each other in the morning.
   b. A teacher and student greet each other in the afternoon.
   c. Two students greet each other in the morning.
   d. Two students greet each other in the afternoon.

2. What situation best describes the conversation between the two speakers?
   a. A teacher and student greet each other in the morning.
   b. A teacher and student greet each other in the afternoon.
   c. Two students greet each other in the morning.
   d. Two students greet each other in the afternoon.

3. What situation best describes the conversation between the two speakers?
   a. A teacher and student exchange goodbyes as they leave.
   b. A teacher and student greet each other when they meet.
   c. Two students exchange goodbyes as they leave.
   d. Two students greet each other when they meet.

4. What situation best describes the conversation between the two speakers?
   a. A teacher and student exchange goodbyes as they leave.
   b. A teacher and student greet each other when they meet.
   c. Two students exchange goodbyes as they leave.
   d. Two students greet each other when they meet.

flip over ⇨

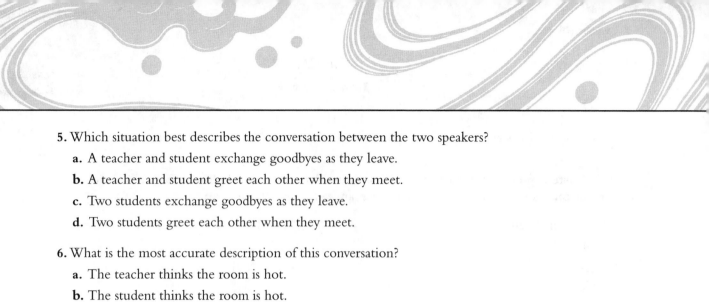

5. Which situation best describes the conversation between the two speakers?

    a. A teacher and student exchange goodbyes as they leave.

    b. A teacher and student greet each other when they meet.

    c. Two students exchange goodbyes as they leave.

    d. Two students greet each other when they meet.

6. What is the most accurate description of this conversation?

    a. The teacher thinks the room is hot.

    b. The student thinks the room is hot.

    c. The student thinks the room is cool.

    d. The student thinks the room is cold.

C You will listen once to a series of conversations. Each question below refers to a different conversation. Choose the most appropriate answer to each question.

1. What page number is it?	2. What page number is it?	3. What page number is it?
a. 56	**a.** 24	**a.** 94
b. 65	**b.** 43	**b.** 48
c. 86	**c.** 34	**c.** 93
d. 58	**d.** 68	**d.** 39

D You will listen once to a series of conversations. Each question below refers to a different conversation. Choose the most appropriate answer to each question.

1. What kind of weather is it?	2. What kind of weather is it?	3. What kind of weather is it?
a. hot	**a.** hot	**a.** hot
b. cold	**b.** cold	**b.** cold
c. cool	**c.** cool	**c.** cool

E You will listen once to a conversation. Choose the most appropriate answer to each question.

1. Who is absent?	2. Who is tardy?
a. Lisa	**a.** Emi
b. Ben	**b.** Mari
c. Jon	**c.** Ben
d. Mike	**d.** Ken

You may not know all the Japanese you hear, but use what you do know along with your imagination!

A **You will listen once to a conversation between a teacher and her students. Choose the most appropriate answer to each question.**

1. Who is speaking loudly?
   a. Ken
   b. Emi
   c. Mike
   d. All of the students

2. Who was asked to read for the class?
   a. Ken
   b. Emi
   c. Mike
   d. All of the above

3. Who was asked to write something?
   a. Ken
   b. Emi
   c. Mike
   d. All of the above

4. Who was asked to close the door?
   a. Ken
   b. Emi
   c. Mike
   d. The teacher

B **You will listen once to a conversation between a teacher and her students. Choose the most appropriate answer to each question.**

1. Who does the pencil belong to?
   a. Ken
   b. Emi
   c. The teacher
   d. The school

2. Who does the dictionary belong to?
   a. Ken
   b. Emi
   c. The teacher
   d. It belongs to the school.

C **You will listen once to a conversation between a teacher and her students. Choose the most appropriate answer to each question.**

1. What belongs to Mike?
   a. money
   b. backpack
   c. cap
   d. book

2. Who does the eraser belong to?
   a. Ken
   b. Emi
   c. The teacher
   d. Mike

D **You will listen once to a conversation between a teacher and her students. Choose the most appropriate answer to each question.**

1. What did Emi receive from her teacher?
   a. candies
   b. paper
   c. erasers
   d. notebooks

2. What did Ken receive from his teacher?
   a. candies
   b. paper
   c. erasers
   d. notebooks

E You will listen once to a conversation between a teacher and her students. Choose the most appropriate answer to each question.

1. Where is the tissue located?
   a. near the teacher
   b. near Mike
   c. near Emi
   d. away from everyone

2. What is near the teacher?
   a. the tissue
   b. Emi's homework
   c. the paper
   d. a book

3. What is near Ken?
   a. the tissue
   b. Emi's homework
   c. the paper
   d. a book

F You will listen once to a conversation between Ken and Emi. Choose the most appropriate answer to each question.

1. When is Emi's birthday?
   a. March 3rd
   b. August 3rd
   c. August 20th
   d. September 20th

2. When is Ken's birthday?
   a. March 3rd
   b. August 3rd
   c. August 20th
   d. September 20th

3. When is Mike's birthday?
   a. March 3rd
   b. August 3rd
   c. August 20th
   d. September 20th

4. What day of the week is Mike's birthday?
   a. Sunday
   b. Monday
   c. Tuesday
   d. Wednesday

G You will listen once to a conversation between Ken and Emi. Choose the most appropriate answer to each question.

1. What time does Japanese class start?
   a. 8:00
   b. 8:30
   c. 9:00
   d. 9:30

2. What time is it now?
   a. 8:00
   b. 8:30
   c. 9:00
   d. 9:30

Ⓐ **Write the correct family terms in the ( ) using *hiragana*.**

(   )   (   )

(   ) (   )   ME   (   ) (   )

Ⓑ **Write the ages of each family member in *hiragana*, including the numbers.**

1.
   9 years old

   おとうとは (   ) さいです。

2.
   5 years old

   いもうとは (   ) さいです。

3.
   23 years old

   あねは (   ) さいです。

4.
   46 years old

   <ruby>父<rt>ちち</rt></ruby>は (   ) さいです。

C Answer the questions by filling in the blanks with the correct responses, based on the family sketch below. Use *hiragana* in your entire response, including numbers.

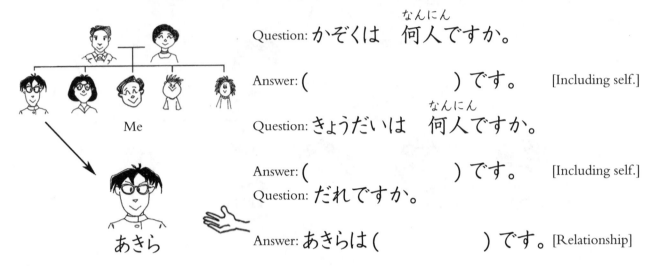

Question: かぞくは　<ruby>何人<rt>なんにん</rt></ruby>ですか。

Answer: (　　　　　　　　　) です。　　[Including self.]

Question: きょうだいは　<ruby>何人<rt>なんにん</rt></ruby>ですか。

Answer: (　　　　　　　　　) です。　　[Including self.]

Question: だれですか。

Answer: あきらは (　　　　　　　) です。[Relationship]

あきら

Me

よみましょう!　Let's read!

<ruby>私<rt>わたし</rt></ruby>の　<ruby>名前<rt>なまえ</rt></ruby>は　かおるです。　かぞくは　<ruby>三人<rt>さんにん</rt></ruby>です。　<ruby>父<rt>ちち</rt></ruby>と　<ruby>母<rt>はは</rt></ruby>と

<ruby>私<rt>わたし</rt></ruby>です。　<ruby>私<rt>わたし</rt></ruby>は　<ruby>十四<rt>じゅうよん</rt></ruby>さいです。　<ruby>父<rt>ちち</rt></ruby>は　<ruby>四十五<rt>よんじゅうご</rt></ruby>さいです。

<ruby>母<rt>はは</rt></ruby>は　<ruby>四十七<rt>よんじゅうなな</rt></ruby>さいです。

Circle the correct answer.

1. What is the writer's name?
   a. Fuuka
   b. Manami
   c. Aina
   d. Kaoru

2. How many siblings does the writer have?
   a. none
   b. 1
   c. 2
   d. 3

3. How old is the writer?
   a. 14
   b. 15
   c. 16
   d. 17

4. How old is the writer's mother?
   a. 42
   b. 45
   c. 47
   d. 54

A This is Keiko's family. Write the correct terms for her family members in the ( ) using *hiragana*.

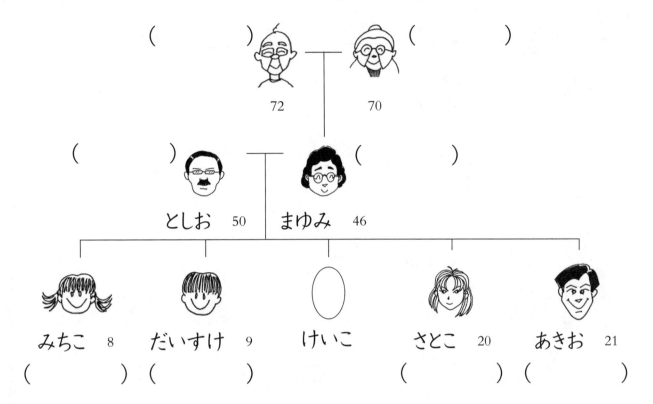

( )   ( )

72   70

( )   ( )

としお 50   まゆみ 46

みちこ 8   だいすけ 9   けいこ   さとこ 20   あきお 21
( )   ( )   ( )   ( )

B Answer the questions based on the information above. Write all numbers in *hiragana*.

1. おねえさんの　名前は　何ですか。　_____ です。

2. お父さんの　名前は　何ですか。　_____ です。

3. お母さんは　何さいですか。　_____ です。

4. おじいさんは　何さいですか。　_____ です。

5. いもうとさんは　何さいですか。　_____ です。

C Fill in the blanks with the correct particles. Choose from は, の, or と.

1. 　ケンさん（　　　）　エミさん（　　　）　16さいです。

   Ken　*Emi*

2. 　お母さん（　　　）　名前（　　　）　まゆみです。

   か あ　　な ま え

3. 　これ（　　　）　私（　　　）　犬 (dog)です。

   わ た し　い ぬ

よみましょう! Let's read!

やまとさんは　十五さいです。　かぞくは　お父さんと　お母さんと

じゅうご　　　　　　　　　　　と う　　　　　か あ

おねえさんと　おばあさんです。　やまとさんの　おねえさんは

二十六さいです。　そして、名前は　あおいです。

にじゅうろく　　　　　　　な ま え

Circle the correct answer.

1. How old is Yamato?
   a. 14
   b. 15
   c. 16
   d. 17

2. Who is Yamato's sibling?
   a. a younger sister
   b. a younger brother
   c. an older sister
   d. an older brother

3. Who is not a member of Yamato's family?
   a. his mother
   b. his father
   c. his grandmother
   d. his grandfather

4. What is the name of Yamato's sibling?
   a. Isami
   b. Aoi
   c. Karina
   d. Naoi

Ⓐ Circle the correct sentence endings based on the information given on the left.

Ken

absent

15 years old

9th grade

Ken
1. ケンさんは 十六さい {A. です B. では ありません}。
(じゅうろく)

Ken
2. ケンさんは 十五さい {A. です B. では ありません}。
(じゅうご)

Ken
3. ケンさんは 中学生 {A. です B. では ありません}。
(ちゅうがくせい)

Ken
4. ケンさんは 高校生 {A. です B. では ありません}。
(こうこうせい)

Ken
5. ケンさんは お休み {A. です B. では ありません}。
(やす)

Ⓑ Use the information below to do Parts a and b.

ケン (Ken) 9th   エミ (Emi) 9th   いくお 10th   アン (Ann) 11th   なおと 12th

a. Complete each statement in *hiragana*.

Ken
1. ケンさんは 何年生ですか。 _____ です。
(なんねんせい)

Emi
2. エミさんは 何年生ですか。 _____ です。
(なんねんせい)

3. いくおさんは 何年生ですか。 _____ です。
(なんねんせい)

An
4. アンさんは 何年生ですか。 _____ です。
(なんねんせい)

5. なおとさんは 何年生ですか。 _____ です。
(なんねんせい)

b. Circle the correct particles based on the information from the previous page.

1. *Ken*
ケンさん { A. は B. の } 中学三年生です。
<small>ちゅうがくさんねんせい</small>

2. *Emi*
エミさん { A. も B. と } 中学三年生です。
<small>ちゅうがくさんねんせい</small>

3. *Ken*
ケンさん { A. は B. も } エミさん { A. と B. も } 中学三年生です。
Emi <small>ちゅうがくさんねんせい</small>

4. *Ken*
ケンさん { A. は B. の } ワシントン 高校 { A. と B. の } 生徒です。
Washinton <small>こうこう</small> <small>せいと</small>

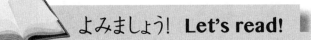 よみましょう! **Let's read!**

だいすけくんは　中学一年生です。　十二さいです。　学校の
<small>ちゅうがくいちねんせい</small> <small>じゅうに</small> <small>がっこう</small>

名前は　すいた中学です。　だいすけくんの　かぞくは　四人です。
<small>なまえ</small> <small>ちゅうがく</small> <small>よにん</small>

お父さんと　お母さんと　おにいさんと　だいすけくんです。
<small>とう</small> <small>かあ</small>

おにいさんは　高校三年生です。　おにいさんの　名前は
<small>こうこう さんねんせい</small> <small>なまえ</small>

ゆうたです。

Circle the correct answer.

1. What grade is Daisuke in?
   a. 7th
   b. 8th
   c. 9th
   d. 10th

2. What is the name of Daisuke's school?
   a. Sakura Intermediate School
   b. Suita Intermediate School
   c. Sakura High School
   d. Suita High School

3. Who is Daisuke's sibling?
   a. a younger sister
   b. a younger brother
   c. an older sister
   d. an older brother

4. What grade is Daisuke's sibling in?
   a. 3rd (elementary)
   b. 8th
   c. 11th
   d. 12th

なまえ *Namae* (Name) _____

ひづけ *Hizuke* (Date) _____ _____ ようび *Yoobi*

(Day of the week)

A どこですか。 **Write in** *hiragana*. **Use** *roomaji* **for #2.**

1.

2.

3.

4.

_____ _____ _____ _____

B 何人ですか。 **Write in** *hiragana*. **Use** *roomaji* **for #3.**
なにじん

1.

2.

3.

4.

_____ _____ _____ _____

C **Match the questions and answers.**

1. 何ですか。（　　）
なん

2. だれですか。（　　）

3. どこですか。（　　）

4. 何月ですか。（　　）
なんがつ

5. 何年生ですか。（　　）
なんねんせい

6. 何日ですか。（　　）
なんにち

7. 何曜日ですか。（　　）
なんようび

A. ゆう子さんです。
こ

B. 水曜日です。
すいようび

C. 中学一年生です。
ちゅうがくいちねんせい

D. 十三日です。
じゅうさんにち

E. 五月です。
ごがつ

F. えんぴつです。

G. あそこです。

D Text Chat: You will participate in a simulated exchange of text-chat messages. Each time it is your turn to write, you should respond as fully and as appropriately as possible. You are having a conversation with a Japanese student for the first time.

1. はじめまして。　私は　なかむらです。　どうぞ　よろしく。

_____

2. 学校は　どこですか。　何年生ですか。

_____

3. ごかぞくは　何人ですか。

_____

4. どうも　ありがとう。　さようなら。

_____

よみましょう！ Let's read!

こちらは　バロー 先生です。　バロー 先生は　フランス人です。

バロー 先生の　おたん生日は　五月九日です。　そして、

四十七さいです。　バロー 先生は　ぼくの　おとうとの

スペイン語の　先生です。

Circle the correct answer.

1. Whose teacher is Mr. Barrow?

  a. younger sister's

  b. younger brother's

  c. older sister's

  d. older brother's

2. When is this teacher's birthday?

  a. April 5

  b. May 9

  c. July 6

  d. September 7

A Circle true (T) or false (F) based on the information below.

| My father is 43 years old. He used to be an engineer, but now he is a doctor. |

1. (T F) 父は　42さいでは　ありません。

2. (T F) 父は　43さいです。

3. (T F) 父は　まえ　エンジニアでした。

4. (T F) 父は　まえ　エンジニアでは　ありませんでした。

5. (T F) 父は　今　いしゃです。

6. (T F) 父は　今　いしゃでは　ありません。

B おしごとは　何ですか。 **Answer in *hiragana*. Write #4 in *roomaji*.**

1.

2.

3.

4.

_____   _____   _____   _____

5.

6.

7.

8.

_____   _____   _____   _____

C Answer based on fact. Write in *hiragana*. Use *roomaji* if appropriate.

Ex. 十八さいですか。

いいえ、十八さいでは ありません。

1. おたん生日は 何月ですか。

_____

2. アメリカ人ですか。

_____

3. お父さんの おしごとは 何ですか。

_____

4. お母さんの おしごとは 何ですか。

_____

 よみましょう! **Let's read!**

父の 名前は けんたです。 父は 今 四十五さいです。

たん生日は 六月です。 父は まえ けいかんでした。

そして、今 べんごしです。

Circle the correct answer.

1. How old is the writer's father?
   a. 45
   b. 49
   c. 50
   d. 54

2. What was the writer's father's job before?
   a. policeman
   b. fireman
   c. engineer
   d. teacher

なまえ *Namae* (Name) _____

ひづけ *Hizuke* (Date) _____ _____ ようび *Yoobi*

(Day of the week)

Introduce your family (including yourself) in Japanese. Attach a photo of your family or draw a picture. Tell how many are in your family, and the names, ages, birthday, jobs, schools, grades, and nationalities of each family member. Use *hiragana* and *roomaji* if appropriate. Use the entire space. Begin and end your paragraph appropriately.

わたしのかぞく

_____

_____

_____

_____

_____

_____

You may not know all the Japanese you hear, but use what you do know along with your imagination!

Ⓐ You will listen once to a conversation between Ken and Emi. Choose the most appropriate answer to each question.

1. How many people are in Ken's family?
   a. two
   b. three
   c. four
   d. five

2. Who is John?
   a. Ken's father
   b. Ken's older brother
   c. Ken's younger brother
   d. Ken's friend

3. How old is Ken's mother?
   a. 45
   b. 44
   c. 43
   d. 42

4. What is Ken's mother's name?
   a. Emi
   b. Hiromi
   c. Mimi
   d. Hiroshi

Ⓑ You will listen once to Emi introduce herself. Choose the most appropriate answer to each question.

1. How many siblings does Emi have?
   a. one
   b. two
   c. three
   d. four

2. How old is Emi's father?
   a. 53
   b. 52
   c. 51
   d. 50

3. Who is Sachiko?
   a. Emi's mother
   b. Emi's older sister
   c. Emi's younger sister
   d. Emi's friend

4. How old is Emi's brother?
   a. 5 years old
   b. 6 years old
   c. 9 years old
   d. 16 years old

Ⓒ You will listen once to a conversation. Choose the most appropriate answer to each question.

1. Which person in Lee's family is not American?
   a. Lee
   b. Lee's mother
   c. Lee's father
   d. Lee's sister

2. Which statement is true?
   a. Lee is the only American in his family.
   b. Lee's mother and Lee are American.
   c. Lee's father and Lee are American.
   d. Everyone in Lee's family is American.

D You will listen once to a conversation. Choose the most appropriate answer to each question.

1. When is Tom's birthday?
   a. January 9
   b. July 9
   c. April 10
   d. September 8

2. When is Akemi's birthday?
   a. January 9
   b. July 9
   c. April 10
   d. September 8

E You will listen once to a conversation. Choose the most appropriate answer to each question.

1. What grade is Tanaka in?
   a. 9th
   b. 10th
   c. 11th
   d. 12th

2. What grade is Mike in?
   a. 9th
   b. 10th
   c. 11th
   d. 12th

F You will listen once to a conversation. Choose the most appropriate answer to each question.

1. What is Dan's father's occupation?
   a. doctor
   b. firefighter
   c. teacher
   d. company employee

2. What is Dan's mother's occupation?
   a. doctor
   b. housewife
   c. teacher
   d. company employee

3. What is Yumi's father's occupation?
   a. doctor
   b. firefighter
   c. teacher
   d. chef

4. What was Yumi's mother's previous occupation?
   a. doctor
   b. housewife
   c. teacher
   d. company employee

5. Who is a waitress?
   a. Yumi
   b. Yumi's mother
   c. Dan's mother
   d. Yumi's sister

6. Who is a chef?
   a. Dan
   b. Dan's father
   c. Dan's brother
   d. Yumi's brother

Ⓐ Respond negatively to each question.

Ex.「わかりますか。」「いいえ、＿＿＿＿わかりません＿＿＿。」

1.「見えますか。」「いいえ、＿＿＿＿＿＿＿＿＿＿＿。」

2.「きこえますか。」「いいえ、＿＿＿＿＿＿＿＿＿＿＿。」

Ⓑ Choose from the particles は, の, を, and で based on the information below.

I do not speak Japanese at home, but I speak a little at school. My friend speaks Japanese well.

1. 私（　）　うち（　）　日本語（　）　はなしません。

でも、学校（　）　すこし　日本語（　）　はなします。

2. 私（　）　ともだち（　）　日本語（　）　よく　はなします。

Ⓒ Circle the correct adverb based on the information below.

My older sister speaks Japanese well. I speak a little Japanese.

1. あねは　日本語を {よく　すこし} はなします。

2. 私は　日本語を {よく　すこし} はなします。

Ⓓ Circle the correct sentence conjunction based on the information below.

My grandmother speaks Japanese well, but she does not speak English well. My grandfather speaks both Japanese and English well.

1. おばあさんは　日本語を　よく　はなします。

{そして　でも}、　えい語を　よく　はなしません。

2. おじいさんは　日本語を　よく　はなします。

{そして　でも}、　えい語も　よく　はなします。

E Answer the question based on fact.

お父さんと　お母さんは　日本語を　はなしますか。

_____

よみましょう!　Let's read!

ぼくの　名前は　とおるです。　かぞくは　三人です。

父と　母と　ぼくです。　父は　けいかんです。　そして、母は

えい語と　日本語を　よく　はなします。　でも、ぼくは

えい語を　はなしません。

Circle the correct answer.

1. How many siblings does the writer have?

   a. none

   b. 1

   c. 2

   d. 3

2. Who can speak English best in the writer's family?

   a. the writer's father

   b. the writer's mother

   c. the writer's sibling

   d. the writer

名前 _____

日づけ _____ _____ 曜日

A 何_{なん}ですか。 **Write in** *hiragana*.

tea

1._____ 2._____ 3._____ 4._____

B **Fill in the blank with** 食_たべます, のみます **or** はなします.

1. 私_{わたし}は 日本語_{ほんご}を _____。

2. 父_{ちち}は 毎_{まい}日 コーヒー_{koohii}を _____。

3. 私_{わたし}の かぞくは 毎_{まい}日 ごはんを _____。

C **Circle the correct adverb based on the information below.**

My family usually eats bread, but sometimes eats rice. I usually drink juice, but sometimes I drink milk.

1. かぞくは { ときどき　たいてい　いつも } パン_{pan}を　食_たべます。

でも、{ ときどき　たいてい　いつも } ごはんを　食_たべます。

2. ぼくは { ときどき　たいてい　いつも } ジュース_{juusu}を　のみます。

でも、{ ときどき　たいてい　いつも } 牛_{ぎゅう}にゅうを　のみます。

D Fill in each blank with the correct particle. Use X if no particle is required.

1. 私_{わたし}（　　　）　毎日_{まい}（　　　）　お水_{みず}（　　　）　のみます。

2. 「コーラ_{koora}（　　　）　のみますか。」

　　「いいえ、コーラ_{koora}（　　　）　のみません。」

3. 私_{わたし}（　　　）かぞく（　　　）

　　うち（　　　）　えい語_ご（　　　）　はなします。

E Answer the questions based on fact.

1. 毎日_{まい}　ごはんを　食_たべますか。　_____

2. ときどき　おちゃを　のみますか。　_____

3. うちで　日本語_{ほんご}を　はなしますか。　_____

よみましょう！ Let's read!

山田_{やまだ}さんは　あさごはんに　たいてい　ごはんを　食_たべます。　でも、

ときどき　パン_{pan}を　食_たべます。　いつも　おちゃを　のみます。　でも、

コーヒー_{koohii}は　のみません。　ときどき　牛_{ぎゅう}にゅうを　のみます。

Circle the correct answer.

1. What does Yamada usually eat for breakfast?

　a. bread

　b. cereal

　c. rice

　d. none of the above

2. What does Yamada always drink with breakfast?

　a. water

　b. milk

　c. juice

　d. tea

A **Here is a chart of Ken's meals for yesterday, today and tomorrow. (X means he didn't eat.)**

	Breakfast	Lunch	Dinner
Yesterday		X	
Today	X NOW		
Tomorrow			

It is now before lunch time, but after breakfast. Fill in each blank with きょう or きのう or あした. Then circle the correct verb form.

ケンさんは

1. _____ あさごはんに　ごはんを { 食べます　食べました }。

2. _____ ひるごはんに　何も { 食べました　食べませんでした }。

3. _____ ばんごはんに　カレー^{karee}を { 食べます　食べました }。

4. _____ あさごはんに　何も { 食べました　食べませんでした }。

5. _____ ひるごはんに　ピザ^{piza}を { 食べます　食べました }。

6. _____ あさごはんに　パン^{pan}を { 食べます　食べました }。

7. _____ ばんごはんに　天ぷらを { 食べます　食べました }。

B Answer the following questions about you and the meals you have eaten.
Answer based on fact.

1. きのう　ばんごはんに　何を　食べましたか。

_____

2. 今日　あさごはんに　何を　のみましたか。

_____

3. 毎日　おひるごはんに　何を　食べますか。

_____

 よみましょう！　**Let's read!**

あねは　きのう　ばんごはんに　天ぷらと　ごはんを　食べました。

そして、　今日　あさごはんに　むすびを　二つ　食べました。　でも、

おひるごはんに　何も　食べませんでした。

Circle the correct answer.

1. When did the writer's sister eat *tempura*?

　　a. lunch yesterday

　　b. dinner yesterday

　　c. lunch today

　　d. dinner today

2. What meal did the writer's sister skip?

　　a. today's breakfast

　　b. today's lunch

　　c. today's dinner

　　d. none

名前 _____

日づけ _____ _____ 曜日

A Fill in each blank with the correct verb chosen from the list below. Use each verb once only.

> はなします　食(た)べます　のみます　よみます
> ききます　します　べんきょうします

1. 私(わたし)は　あさ　しんぶんを　_____。

2. いつも　おんがくを　_____。

3. あさごはんに　パン(pan)を　_____。

4. 牛(ぎゅう)にゅうを　_____。

5. 学校(がっこう)で　日本語(ほんご)を　_____。

6. としょかんで　しゅくだいを　_____。

7. うちで　おばあさんと　日本語(ほんご)を　_____。

B Fill in each blank with the correct particle. Write X where there should be no particle.

1. カフェテリア(kafeteria)（　　）　おひるごはん（　　）　食(た)べました。

2. 今日(きょう)（　　）　おひるごはん（　　）ハンバーガー(hanbaagaa)（　　）食(た)べました。

3. ぼく（　　）　ともだち（　　）　いっしょ（　　）　食(た)べました。

4. でも、ぼく（　　）　ときどき（　　）　何(なに)（　　）　食(た)べません。

C Matching: Choose the correct answer from the box at the right. Use each answer only once.

_____ 1. どこですか。

_____ 2. 何^{なん}ですか。

_____ 3. だれですか。

_____ 4. 何年生^{なんねんせい}ですか。

_____ 5. いくつですか。

_____ 6. 何人^{なんにん}ですか。

_____ 7. 何月^{なんがつ}ですか。

A. 先生^{せんせい}です。

B. 中学三年生^{ちゅうがく ねんせい}です。

C. 十月^{じゅうがつ}です。

D. 一人^{ひとり}です。

E. 一つ　ください。

F. ざっしです。

G. としょかんです。

 よみましょう!　**Let's read!**

私^{わたし}は　今日^{きょう}　ゆみさんと　おひるごはんを　しょくどうで

食^たべました。　ゆみさんと　私^{わたし}は　おべんとうを　食^たべました。

ゆみさんと　私^{わたし}は　お水^{みず}を　のみました。

Circle the correct answer.

1. When did the writer eat with his/her friend?

   a. breakfast yesterday

   b. lunch yesterday

   c. breakfast today

   d. lunch today

2. Where did the writer eat with his/her friend?

   a. at the snack bar

   b. at the cafeteria

   c. outside

   d. in the classroom

A これは 何^{なん}ですか。 **Answer in** *hiragana.*

1._____ 2._____ 3._____ 4._____

B どこですか。 **Answer in** *hiragana.*

1._____ 2._____ 3._____ 4._____

C Fill in each blank with the correct particle based on the information below. Write X where there should be no particle.

> I usually do my homework at the library. But today I studied English with my friend. I typed my English paper using a computer at the computer lab.

私^{わたし}（ 　 ）　たいてい（ 　 ）　としょかん（ 　 ）　しゅくだい（ 　 ）

します。 でも、 今日^{きょう}（ 　 ）　としょかん（ 　 ）

ともだち（ 　 ）　えい語^ご（ 　 ）　べんきょうしました。 私^{わたし}（ 　 ）

konpyuutaarabo
コンピューターラボ（ 　 ）　えい語^ご（ 　 ）　*repooto*
レポート（ 　 ）

pasokon
パソコン（ 　 ）　*taipu*
タイプしました。

D Fill in each blank with the correct verb from the list below. Change the verb to past tense. Use each verb once only.

はなします　食べます　のみます　よみます　ききます　見ます　かきます

1. きのうの　ばん　テレビを _____。

2. そして、ラジオを _____。

3. えい語の　本を _____。

4. そして、よる　手がみを _____。

5. でんわで　ともだちと _____。

6. おむすびを _____。

7. そして、おちゃを _____。

よみましょう！　Let's read!

きのうは　木曜日でしたが、　みどりさんは　ばん　うちで　何も

しませんでした。　五人の　ともだちと　フェイスブックで　よく

はなしました。　でも、　えい語の　しゅくだいを　しませんでした。

Circle the correct answer.

1. What day of the week is it today?
   a. Thursday
   b. Friday
   c. Saturday
   d. Sunday

2. What was last night like for Midori?
   a. productive
   b. lazy
   c. exhausting
   d. miserable

You may not know all the Japanese you hear, but use your best knowledge and imagination!

A **You will listen once to a conversation between Ken and Emi. Choose the most appropriate answer to each question.**

1. Who speaks Japanese well in Ken's family?
   a. Ken
   b. Ken's father
   c. Ken's mother
   d. nobody in his family

2. Who does not speak Japanese at all?
   a. Emi's father
   b. Ken's father
   c. Ken's mother
   d. Emi's mother

B **You will listen once to a narrative about Li. Choose the most appropriate answer to each question.**

1. How old is Li?
   a. 13
   b. 14
   c. 15
   d. 16

2. What is Li's nationality?
   a. Japanese
   b. Chinese
   c. Korean
   d. American

3. What language does Li speak at home?
   a. Japanese
   b. Chinese
   c. Korean
   d. English

4. What grade is Li?
   a. 9th
   b. 10th
   c. 11th
   d. 12th

C **You will listen once to a conversation between Ken and Emi. Choose the most appropriate answer to each question.**

1. What does Ken's family usually eat?
   a. rice
   b. bread
   c. beef
   d. vegetables

2. What do Emi's parents always eat ?
   a. rice
   b. bread
   c. beef
   d. vegetables

D **You will listen once to a narrative about a person. Choose the most appropriate answer to each question.**

1. Who is this passage about?
   a. the speaker's mother
   b. the speaker's father
   c. the speaker's grandmother
   d. the speaker's grandfather

2. How old is the person spoken about?
   a. 60
   b. 62
   c. 64
   d. 65

flip over ⇨

3. What did this person do for a career?

   a. doctor

   b. lawyer

   c. engineer

   d. teacher

4. What does this person drink?

   a. coffee and tea

   b. tea and water

   c. tea and milk

   d. coffee and cola

E You will listen once to a conversation between Ken and Emi. Choose the most appropriate answer to each question.

1. Who eats breakfast everyday?

   a. Emi

   b. Ken

   c. both Emi and Ken

   d. neither Emi nor Ken

2. What did Ken eat this morning?

   a. nothing

   b. rice and fish

   c. rice, eggs and ham

   d. bread, eggs and ham

3. What did Ken drink this morning? Choose two.

   a. tea

   b. milk

   c. juice

   d. water

4. What did Emi eat this morning?

   a. nothing

   b. rice and fish

   c. rice, eggs and ham

   d. bread, eggs and ham

F You will listen once to a conversation between Ken and Emi. Choose the most appropriate answer to each question.

1. Where does Emi usually eat lunch?

   a. in the classroom

   b. at the cafeteria

   c. at the snack bar

   d. outside

2. With whom does Emi eat lunch?

   a. Ken

   b. another friend

   c. with her teacher

   d. she eats alone

3. When is/was the Japanese exam?

   a. yesterday

   b. today

   c. tomorrow

   d. day after tomorrow

4. What will Emi do today?

   a. She will read a book.

   b. She will watch a movie.

   c. She will write her report.

   d. She will study for her Japanese test.

A Write the answers in *hiragana* using the cue words in your responses. Make appropriate changes to the subjects of the sentences.

Ex. お父さんの　しゅみは　何ですか。(music)

（　　ちち　　）の　しゅみは（　　　　おんがく　　　　　　）です。

1. お母さんの　しゅみは　何ですか。(singing)

（　　　　　　）の　しゅみは（　　　　　　　　　　　）です。

2. おねえさんの　しゅみは　何ですか。(movies and reading)

（　　　　　　）の　しゅみは（　　　　　　　　　　　）です。

3. おにいさんの　しゅみは　何ですか。(swimming)

（　　　　　　）の　しゅみは（　　　　　　　　　　　）です。

4. あなたの　しゅみは　何ですか。(painting and movies)

（　　　　　　）の　しゅみは（　　　　　　　　　　　）です。

5. おとうとさんの　しゅみは　何ですか。(video games)

（　　　　　　）の　しゅみは（　　　　　　　　　　　）です。

6. おじいさんの　しゅみは　何ですか。(playing cards and jogging)

（　　　　　　）の　しゅみは（　　　　　　　　　　　）です。

B Describe your family members' hobbies, including your own, in Japanese.

_____

_____

_____

_____

_____

 よみましょう! **Let's read!**

Circle the correct answer based on the reading.

1. How old is the writer's grandmother?

   a. 56

   b. 57

   c. 65

   d. 68

2. What does the writer's grandmother do in the morning?

   a. She talks to her friends.

   b. She reads.

   c. She writes letters.

   d. She enjoys music.

3. What does his/her grandmother do in the afternoon?

   a. She takes a nap at home.

   b. She reads books at home.

   c. She reads books at the library.

   d. She talks to her friend.

4. How does the writer interact with his/her grandmother?

   a. The writer lives with his/her grandmother.

   b. The writer talks to his/her grandmother daily.

   c. The writer sometimes talks to his/her grandmother on the phone.

   d. The writer doesn't talk to his/her grandmother much.

わたしの　おばあさんは　六十五さいです。
おばあさんの　しゅみは　おんがくと　どくしょ
です。おばあさんは　毎日　あさ　うちで
クラシック _kurashikku_ の　CDを　ききます。
そして、おひる　としょかんで　本を　よみます。
わたしは　ときどき　おばあさんと　でんわで
はなします。

名前 _____

日づけ _____ _____ 曜日

Ⓐ Circle はい or いいえ according to your preference. Then write an appropriate follow-up sentence in Japanese using 好き.

Ex. おすしが　好きですか。

（はい　（いいえ））、おすしが　好きでは　ありません。 _____

1. スポーツ（*supootsu*）が　好きですか。

（はい　いいえ）、_____

2. どくしょが　好きですか。

（はい　いいえ）、_____

Ⓑ Fill in the blanks with the correct tense endings using the English statements as cues.

A.

I used to like baseball before, but now I do not like baseball. I like football now.

ぼくは　まえ　やきゅうが　好き_____。

でも、今（*いま*）　やきゅうは　好き_____。

今（*いま*）　フットボール（*futtobooru*）が　好き_____。

B.

Emi did not like sushi before, but now she likes it.

エミ（*Emi*）さんは　まえ　おすしが　好き_____。

でも、今（*いま*）　おすしが　好き_____。

C Write your own answers in Japanese in the blanks, then circle the correct word from the choices in the {   }.

1. どんな　のみものが　好^すきですか。

   そうですねえ...　私^{わたし}は＿＿＿＿＿が｛好^すき　大好^{だいす}き｝です。

2. どんな　食^たべものが　きらいですか。

   そうですねえ...　私^{わたし}は＿＿＿＿が｛きらい　大^{だい}きらい｝です。

3. 学校^{がっこう}が　好^すきですか。

   ｛はい　いいえ｝、学校^{がっこう}が｛好^すき　大好^{だいす}き　きらい　大^{だい}きらい｝です。

 よみましょう！　**Let's read!**

Circle the correct answer based on the reading.

1. What grade is Daisuke in?
   a. 7th grade
   b. 8th grade
   c. 9th grade
   d. 10th grade

2. Which statement best describes Daisuke?
   a. Daisuke likes to study.
   b. Daisuke loves playing video games.
   c. Daisuke does homework everyday.
   d. Daisuke is a good student.

わたしの　おとうとの　名前は
だいすけです。おとうとは　ちゅう
がく一ねんせいです。テレビゲーム
terebigeemu が　だいすきです。でも、
べんきょうが　だいきらいです。しゅ
くだいを　しません。だめですねえ。

A Conjoin the two sentences using が "but." Then translate the whole sentence into English.

Ex. 私_{わたし}は　サッカー_{sakkaa}が　好_すきです。　でも、上手_{じょうず}では　ありません。

→ 私_{わたし}は　サッカー_{sakkaa}が　好_すきですが、上手_{じょうず}では　ありません。

English: I like soccer, but I am not skillful at it.

1. 父_{ちち}は　水_{すい}えいが　上手_{じょうず}です。　でも、母_{はは}は　下手_{へた}です。

→ _____

English: _____

2. あねは　どくしょが　大好_{だいす}きです。　でも、あには　大_{だい}きらいです。

→ _____

English: _____

3. おとうとは　えが　とくいです。　でも、私_{わたし}は　にが手_てです。

→ _____

English: _____

B Write your answers based on fact. Remember that humility is highly valued in Japanese culture.

1. 日本語_{ほんご}が　上手_{じょうず}ですか。

_____

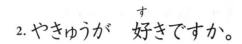

2. やきゅうが　好_すきですか。

3. やきゅうが　上手_{じょうず}ですか。

4. どんな　ことが　とくいですか。

5. どんな　ことが　にが手_てですか。

 よみましょう! **Let's read!**

Circle the correct answer based on the reading.

1. Who is good at baseball?
   a. the writer's father
   b. the writer's mother
   c. the writer's sibling
   d. none of the above

2. Who is good at swimming?
   a. the writer's mother
   b. the writer's father
   c. the writer's sibling
   d. none of the above

3. How many people are there in the writer's family, including himself/herself?
   a. 3
   b. 4
   c. 5
   d. 6

ちちは　ゴルフ *gorufu* が　だいすきですが、じょうずでは　ありません。ははは　テニス *tenisu* が　すきです。そして、じょうずです。あねは　テニス *tenisu* が　とくいですが、水えいが　にがてです。おとうとは　やきゅうが　とくいです。

A **Fill in the (   ) with the correct adverbs based on the English information below. Finish the sentences using appropriate endings.**

Taroo is very good at baseball. He is "so-so" at golf. He is a little skillful at basketball. He is not very good at soccer. He cannot swim at all.

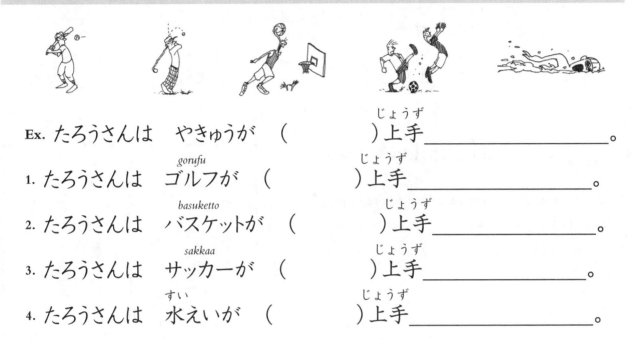

Ex. たろうさんは　やきゅうが　（　　　　　）上手＿＿＿＿＿＿＿＿＿＿。
じょうず

1. たろうさんは　ゴルフが　（　　　　　）上手＿＿＿＿＿＿＿＿＿。
gorufu じょうず

2. たろうさんは　バスケットが　（　　　　　）上手＿＿＿＿＿＿＿。
basuketto じょうず

3. たろうさんは　サッカーが　（　　　　　）上手＿＿＿＿＿＿＿。
sakkaa じょうず

4. たろうさんは　水えいが　（　　　　　）上手＿＿＿＿＿＿＿。
すい じょうず

B **Circle** はい **or** いいえ **based on your opinion and write one of the adverbs in the box below in the (　　). You may use each more than once. Then complete the sentence with the correct ending.**

とても　まあまあ　すこし　ぜんぜん　あまり

1. すもうが　好きですか。
す

(はい　いいえ)、すもうが（　　　　　）好き＿＿＿＿＿＿＿＿＿。
す

2. 学校が　好きですか。
がっこう す

(はい　いいえ)、学校が（　　　　　）好き＿＿＿＿＿＿＿＿。
がっこう す

3. え が 　上手（じょうず）ですか。

　　（はい　いいえ）、え が（　　　　　　　　　）上手（じょうず）＿＿＿＿＿＿＿＿＿＿＿。

4. 日本語（にほんご）が　上手（じょうず）ですか。

　　（はい　いいえ）、日本語（にほんご）ごが（　　　　　　　　　）上手（じょうず）＿＿＿＿＿＿＿＿＿＿。

 よみましょう!　**Let's read!**

Circle the correct answer based on the reading.

1. How old is Makiko?
   a. 14
   b. 15
   c. 16
   d. 17

2. What grade is Makiko?
   a. freshman
   b. sophomore
   c. junior
   d. senior

3. What does Makiko dislike?
   a. school
   b. studying
   c. soccer
   d. none of the above

まきこさんは　十五さいです。
そして、こうこう一ねんせいです。
サッカー*sakkaa* が　だいすきです。
がっこうで　まい日　サッカー*sakkaa*
をします。がっこうが　だいすきで
すが、べんきょうは　あまり　すき
ではありません。

名前 _____

日づけ _____ _____ 曜日

A **Color the picture as described below.**

これは　ぼくの　うちです。　ぼくの　うちは　ちゃいろです。

ピアノは　くろです。　ギターは　きいろです。　でんわは　あかです。
piano　　　　　　　　　　　*gitaa*

ぼくの　ぼうしは　むらさきです。　ぼくの　シャツは　あおです。
　　　　　　　　　　　　　　　　　　　　　　　　　　　　shatsu

*ズボンは　くろです。　そして、　ソックスは　白です。
zubon　　　　　　　　　　　　*sokkusu*　　　　しろ

犬は　白と　くろです。　ぼくの　リュックは　みどりです。
いぬ　しろ　　　　　　　　　　　　　*ryukku*

*ズボン: pants
zubon

B Fill in the blanks in Japanese with appropriate color words.

1. 私_{わたし}の　学校_{がっこう}の　いろは＿＿＿＿＿＿＿と＿＿＿＿＿＿＿です。

2. この　かみの　いろは＿＿＿＿＿＿＿です。

3. チョコレートの　いろは　たいてい＿＿＿＿＿＿です。
   chokoreeto

4. ごはんの　いろは　たいてい＿＿＿＿＿＿です。

5. オレンジジュースの　いろは＿＿＿＿＿＿です。
   orenjijuusu

6. 牛_{ぎゅう}にゅうの　いろは＿＿＿＿＿＿です。

7. 日本の　おちゃの　いろは　たいてい＿＿＿＿＿＿です。
   ほん

8. 日本の　はた(flag)の　いろは＿＿＿＿＿と＿＿＿＿です。
   ほん

9. アメリカの　はた(flag)の　いろは＿＿＿と＿＿＿と＿＿＿です。
   amerika

C Write your answers in Japanese.

1. 何_{なに}いろが　好_すきですか。　そして、何_{なに}いろが　きらいですか。

＿＿＿＿＿＿＿＿＿＿＿＿＿＿＿＿＿＿＿＿＿＿＿＿＿＿＿＿＿

2. むらさきの　いろが　好_すきですか。

＿＿＿＿＿＿＿＿＿＿＿＿＿＿＿＿＿＿＿＿＿＿＿＿＿＿＿＿＿

名前 _____

日づけ _____ _____ 曜日

You may not know all the Japanese you hear, but use what you do know along with your imagination!

A **You will listen once to a conversation between Ken and Emi. Choose the most appropriate answer to each question.**

1. What are Ken's hobbies?

   a. skateboarding and playing the guitar

   b. surfing and playing the guitar

   c. swimming and playing the guitar

   d. playing the guitar and video games

2. What are Emi's hobbies?

   a. dancing and movies

   b. music and movies

   c. music and painting

   d. reading and music

B **You will listen once to a narrative about Ken's family. Choose the most appropriate answer to each question.**

1. How many people are in Ken's family, including Ken?

   a. two

   b. three

   c. four

   d. five

2. Which statement is true about Ken's family?

   a. Ken has one older sister.

   b. Ken has one older brother.

   c. Ken's father's hobby is reading.

   d. Ken's mother's hobby is golf.

C **You will listen once to a conversation between Ken and Emi. Choose the most appropriate answer to each question.**

1. How well does Ken like sushi?

   a. He likes it a little.

   b. He likes it very much.

   c. He does not like it much.

   d. He does not like it at all.

2. Who likes pizza?

   a. Ken only

   b. Emi only

   c. Both Ken and Emi

   d. Neither Ken nor Emi

D **You will listen once to a narrative about a person. Choose the most appropriate answer to each question.**

1. Who is 60 years old?

   a. the speaker's mother

   b. the speaker's grandmother

   c. the speaker's father

   d. the speaker's grandfather

2. Which statement is not true?

   a. The person described likes dancing.

   b. The person described likes Japanese food.

   c. The person described does not like American food.

   d. The person described drinks tea everyday.

E You will listen once to a narrative. Choose the most appropriate answer to each question.

1. Which persons are proficient in Japanese?
   a. the speaker's grandparents
   b. the speaker's grandmother and mother
   c. the speaker's mother and older sister
   d. the speaker's grandfather and older sister

2. Who does not speak Japanese at all?
   a. the speaker's grandmother
   b. the speaker's mother
   c. the speaker's older sister
   d. the speaker

F You will listen once to a narrative. Choose the most appropriate answer to each question.

1. Which sport is the speaker good at?
   a. baseball
   b. football
   c. soccer
   d. tennis

2. Which sport is the speaker poor at?
   a. baseball
   b. football
   c. soccer
   d. tennis

G You will listen once to a conversation between Ken and Emi. Choose the most appropriate answer or answers to each question. You may choose more than one answer in this section.

1. What is Emi's favorite color?
   a. red
   b. yellow
   c. blue
   d. green

2. What is Ken's favorite color?
   a. red
   b. yellow
   c. blue
   d. green

3. What colors does Emi dislike? Choose two answers.
   a. red
   b. white
   c. purple
   d. green

4. What colors does Ken dislike? Choose two answers.
   a. red
   b. green
   c. black
   d. brown

名前 _____

日づけ _____ _____ 曜日

A **Answer the questions according to the picture below.**

<ruby>父<rt>ちち</rt></ruby>　<ruby>母<rt>はは</rt></ruby>　あに　あね

a. Circle the correct answer.

1. おねえさんは　せが　{ A.たかい　　B.ひくい } です。

2. おじいさんは　せが　{ A.たかい　　B.ひくい } です。

3. いもうとさんは　せが　{ A.たかい　　B.ひくい } です。

b. Circle the correct answer.

1. おにいさんは　せが　{ A.とても　　B.ちょっと　　C.まあまあ } たかいです。

2. お<ruby>母<rt>かあ</rt></ruby>さんは　せが　　{ A.とても　　B.ちょっと } ひくいです。

3. おとうとさんは　せが　{ A.とても　　B.ちょっと } ひくいです。

c. Complete the sentences to describe each person's height using the cue words given.

1. (a little tall)

　　お<ruby>父<rt>とう</rt></ruby>さんは _____。

2. (a little short)

　　お<ruby>母<rt>かあ</rt></ruby>さんは _____。

3. (very tall)

おにいさんは　_____。

4. (very short)

おとうとさんは　_____。

5. (a little tall)

おじいさんは　_____。

B **Write the names of each body part in *hiragana*.**

head

face

body

A Answer the questions according to the pictures below.

あきら　　けんじ　　おじいさん　　ゆみ　　たかし　　みき　　とおる

a. Circle the correct answers.

1. あきらさんは　せが　{ A. たかい　B. ひくい } です。

2. おじいさんは　目_めが　{ A. いい　B. わるい } です。

3. とおるさんは　かみのけが　{ A. ながい　B. みじかい } です。

b. Circle the correct answers.

1. おじいさんは　目_めが　{ A. 良_よくないです　B. わるくないです }。

2. ゆみさんの　ぼうしは　{ A. 大_{おお}きくないです　B. 小_{ちい}さくないです }。

3. みきさんは　かみのけが　{ A. ながくないです　B. みじかくないです }。

c. Answer with a negative verb ending in your reply.

Ex. けんじさんは　せが　たかいですか。

いいえ、たかくないです。 or _いいえ、たかくありません。_

1. あきらさんは　せが　ひくいですか。

_____

2. たかしさんの　ぼうしは　大_{おお}きいですか。

_____

3. みきさんは　かみのけが　みじかいですか。

_____

B Write your answers based on fact using an adverb from the box below.

> とても　ちょっと　まあまあ　あまり　ぜんぜん

1. せが　たかいですか。_____

2. 目_めが　いいですか。_____

3. 目_めが　大_{おお}きいですか。_____

4. かみのけが　ながいですか。_____

5. あたまが　いいですか。_____

よみましょう!　Let's read!

Circle the correct answer based on the reading.

1. What grade is the writer's brother?
   a. 9th
   b. 10th
   c. 11th
   d. 12th

2. What sports can the writer's brother play well?
   a. good at soccer, but not good at baseball
   b. good at baseball, but not good at soccer
   c. good at soccer and baseball
   d. not good at soccer and baseball

3. What kind of student is his/her brother?
   a. very smart, but does not study
   b. smart and studies well
   c. not smart, but studies hard
   d. not smart and does not study

> ぼくの　あには　こうこう三ねんせいです。あには　せが　とても　たかいです。そして、スポーツ supootsu が とくいです。サッカー sakkaa が じょうずですが、やきゅうは　あまり　じょうずでは　ありません。あには　あまり　あたまが　よくないです。べんきょうも　あまり　しません。

A Answer using the cue words given.

Ex. かみのけは　何_{なに}いろですか。(black)　　くろいです。　or くろです。

1. けしごむは　何_{なに}いろですか。(yellow)　　_____ or _____

2. 目_めは　何_{なに}いろですか。(brown)　　_____ or _____

3. ぼうしは　何_{なに}いろですか。(white and blue)　_____

B Answer the questions using negative ending responses.

Ex. うちは　白_{しろ}いですか。

いいえ、(　　　　　しろくないです　　　　)。

1. 目_めは　あおいですか。

いいえ、(　　　　　　　　　　　　　)。

2. おじいさんの　かみのけは　くろいですか。

いいえ、(　　　　　　　　　　　　　)。

3. リュックは　みどりですか。
　 ryukku

いいえ、(　　　　　　　　　　　　　)。

4. 学校_{がっこう}の　いろは　きいろと　みどりですか。

いいえ、(　　　　　　　　　　　　　　　)。

C Based on fact, choose an adverb from among とても, すこし, あまり, ぜんぜん, まあまあ, and write it in the (　) and circle the correct ending.

1. 私<ruby>私<rt>わたし</rt></ruby>は　目<ruby>目<rt>め</rt></ruby>が（　　　　　　　　）（大<ruby>大<rt>おお</rt></ruby>きいです　大<ruby>大<rt>おお</rt></ruby>きくないです）。

2. 私<ruby>私<rt>わたし</rt></ruby>の　こえは（　　　　　　　　）（大<ruby>大<rt>おお</rt></ruby>きいです　大<ruby>大<rt>おお</rt></ruby>きくないです）。

3. 私<ruby>私<rt>わたし</rt></ruby>は　せが（　　　　　　）（たかいです　たかくないです）。

4. 私<ruby>私<rt>わたし</rt></ruby>は　かみのけが（　　　　　　）（ながいです　ながくないです）。

5. 私<ruby>私<rt>わたし</rt></ruby>は　あたまが（　　　　　　　）（いいです　良<ruby>良<rt>よ</rt></ruby>くないです）。

D Restate the following in Japanese, then draw a picture of the person as she is described.

1. My mother's hobby is karaoke. She likes singing very much, but she is not good at singing at all. Her voice is bad.

_____

_____

_____

_____

名前 _____

日づけ _____ _____ 曜日

A Answer the questions according to the pictures below.

なかむら　　山田(やまだ)　　三木(みき)　　早川(はやかわ)　　大山(おおやま)　　さとう

a. Choose the correct answers.

1. 山田(やまだ)さんは　{A. 太(ふと)っています　B. やせています }。

2. 早川(はやかわ)さんは　{A. わかいです　B. 年(とし)を　とっています }。

3. 大山先生(おおやませんせい)は　{A. きびしいです　B. やさしいです }。

b. Answer the questions <u>using negative conjugations</u>.

Ex. なかむらさんは　やせていますか。　いいえ、<u>やせていません。</u>

1. 山田(やまだ)さんは　太(ふと)っていますか。　いいえ、_____

2. 三木(みき)さんは　年(とし)を　とっていますか。　いいえ、_____

3. さとう先生(せんせい)は　きびしいですか。　いいえ、_____

B Answer the questions based on fact. <u>Use an adverb in your response</u>. Use the correct sentence ending and the correct subject.

1. お父(とう)さんは　やせていますか。

_____

2. お父(とう)さんは　せが　たかいですか。

_____

3. お父さんは　きびしいですか。

_____

4. お父さんの　目は　いいですか。

_____

5. お父さんは　よく　テレビを　見ますか。

_____

6. お父さんは　ゴルフが　上手ですか。

_____

A Answer the questions based on the pictures below.

あき<ruby>子<rt>こ</rt></ruby>

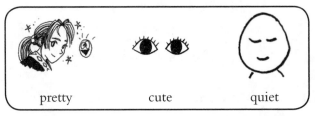

pretty   cute   quiet

一ろう

noisy   dirty   nuisance

a. Circle the correct answers.

1. あき<ruby>子<rt>こ</rt></ruby>さんは　{ A. きれい　　B. きたない } です。

2. あき<ruby>子<rt>こ</rt></ruby>さんは　<ruby>目<rt>め</rt></ruby>が　{ A. かわいい　　B. きれい } です。

3. あき<ruby>子<rt>こ</rt></ruby>さんは　{ A. しずか　　B. うるさい } です。

4. 一ろうさんは　{ A. しずか　　B. うるさい } です。

5. 一ろうさんは　あしが { A. きれい　　B. きたない } です。

6. 一ろうさんは　{ A. やさしい　　B. じゃま } です。

b. Answer the questions using negative ending responses.

Ex. あき<ruby>子<rt>こ</rt></ruby>さんは　うるさいですか。

いいえ、<u>うるさくないです。_____</u>

1. 一ろうさんは　しずかですか。　いいえ、_____

2. 一ろうさんは　あしが　きれいですか。　いいえ、_____

3. あき<ruby>子<rt>こ</rt></ruby>さんは　<ruby>目<rt>め</rt></ruby>が　<ruby>小<rt>ちい</rt></ruby>さいですか。　いいえ、_____

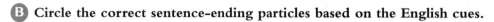

B Circle the correct sentence-ending particles based on the English cues.

1. 「うるさいです (A. ねえ　B. ね　C. よ)。」　　"You are noisy, you know. (Be quiet.)"

　「すみません。」　　"Sorry."

2. 「うるさいです (A. ねえ　B. ね　C. よ)。」　　"It is so noisy!"

　「そうです (A. ねえ　B. ね　C. よ)。」　　"Yes, it is!"

3. 「うるさいです (A. ねえ　B. ね　C. よ)。」　　"It is noisy, isn't it?"

　「そうですね。」

よみましょう！ Let's read!

Circle the correct answer based on the reading.

1. What is the writer's sister like?
   a. a little short and a little plump
   b. very short and a little plump
   c. a little tall and very thin
   d. very tall and a little thin

2. What does the writer think of his/her sister?
   a. cute, but always loud
   b. sometimes loud, but cute
   c. not very cute, but never loud
   d. not very cute, and sometimes loud

3. How is the writer's sister at music?
   a. likes music, but is not talented
   b. has a loud voice, but not good at singing at all
   c. sings loud and well
   d. loves music but doesn't like singing

ぼくの　いもうとの　名前は　ゆかです。四さいです。せが　とても　ひくいです。そして、すこし　ふとっています。ゆかは　かわいいですが、いつも　とても　うるさいです。ぼくの　CDが　だいすきです。そして、じゃまです。ゆかは　うたがだいすきです。こえが　おおきいですが、あまり　じょうずでは　ありません。

You've received a letter from a Japanese student. Write a letter in reply. Include answers to her questions in addition to writing about yourself. Use all of the space provided.

　　　はじめまして。　私は　山田かおりです。　なかむら高校の

二年生です。　あなたは　何年生ですか。　学校の　名前は

何ですか。　私は　学校が　好きですが、あなたも　学校が

好きですか。　私は　えい語を　すこし　はなしますが、あなたは

日本語が　上手ですか。　しゅみは　何ですか。　私は　えいがと

おんがくが　好きです。　私の　えい語の　先生は　とても

きびしいですが、あなたの　日本語の　先生も　きびしいですか。

では、お手がみを　くださいね。

　　　　　　　　　　　　　　　　　　　　さようなら。

11月　1日　　　　　　　　　　　　　　　　山田かおり

_____

_____

_____

_____

_____

_____

_____

You may not know all the Japanese you hear, but use what you do know along with your imagination!

A You will listen once to a conversation between Ken and Emi. Choose the most appropriate answer to each question.

1. Besides Ken, who is tall in his family?
  a. his sister
  b. his father
  c. his brother
  d. his mother

2. Who is short among Ken's family?
  a. Only Ken's sister
  b. Ken's parents
  c. Ken's mother and sister
  d. Ken's father and sister

B You will listen once to a narrative. Choose the most appropriate answer to each question.

1. Who is Yuki?
  a. the speaker
  b. the speaker's older sister
  c. the speaker's younger sister
  d. the speaker's friend

2. Which statement about Yuki is NOT true?
  a. She is a 7th grader.
  b. She is 13 years old.
  c. She is tall.
  d. She is smart.

3. What is the speaker's father's occupation?
  a. doctor
  b. lawyer
  c. teacher
  d. firefighter

4. Which statement about the speaker's father is NOT true?
  a. He is 45 years old.
  b. He is a little short.
  c. He is thin.
  d. He is generous.

C You will listen once to a narrative about family members. Choose the most appropriate answer to each question.

1. Who is Akira?
  a. the speaker's older brother
  b. the speaker's father
  c. the speaker's younger brother
  d. the speaker's friend

2. Which statement is NOT true?
  a. Akira is short.
  b. Akira is noisy.
  c. Akira has black hair.
  d. Akira likes baseball.

D You will listen once to a conversation between Ken and Emi. Choose the most appropriate answer to each question.

1. Who has green eyes?
  a. Ken's mother
  b. Emi
  c. Ken's father
  d. Ken

2. Who has brown eyes?
  a. Ken's mother
  b. Emi
  c. Ken's father
  d. Ken

flip over ⇨

3. Who is 39 years old?

  a. Ken's mother

  b. Emi's mother

  c. Ken's father

  d. Emi's father

4. Which statement is true?

  a. Ken's father is not healthy.

  b. Ken's father is strict.

  c. Ken's mother is strict.

  d. Ken's mother is kind.

E **You will listen once to a narrative. Choose the most appropriate answer to each question.**

1. What does Mr. Smith teach?

  a. Japanese

  b. English

  c. Spanish

  d. Chinese

2. Which statement about Mr. Smith is true?

  a. He is a little tall.

  b. He is a little thin.

  c. He is young.

  d. He is sometimes very strict.

3. Which statement is not true?

  a. Mr. Smith is young.

  b. Mr. Smith is a very good teacher.

  c. Mr. Smith is sometimes strict.

  d. The speaker likes Mr. Smith.

F **You will listen once to a narrative. Choose the most appropriate answer to each question.**

1. Which statement is true?

  a. Scott is kind.

  b. Scott is skilled at Japanese.

  c. Scott is not skilled at sports.

  d. Scott has brown eyes.

2. Which statement is NOT true?

  a. Scott is cute.

  b. Scott can see well.

  c. Scott and the speaker eat lunch together.

  d. The speaker likes Scott.

G **You will listen once to a narrative. Choose the most appropriate answer to each question.**

1. What grade is Arisa in?

  a. 7th

  b. 8th

  c. 9th

  d. 10th

2. Which statement is NOT true?

  a. Arisa is quiet.

  b. Arisa understands English very well.

  c. Arisa studies hard.

  d. Arisa and the speaker are seeing a movie on Saturday.

名前 _____

日づけ _____ _____ 曜日

Ⓐ なんじですか。 **Answer in** *hiragana.*

Ex.

いちじにふん です。

1.

_____ です。

2.

_____ です。

3.

_____ です。

4.

_____ です。

5.

_____ です。

Ⓑ なんじですか。 **Answer in** *hiragana.*

Ex.   9:30

くじはん です。

1.   about 8:00

_____ です。

2.   about 1:30

_____ です。

3.   before 1:00

_____ です。

4.   after 3:00

_____ です。

5.   5 minutes before 7

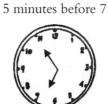

_____ です。

C Make the following suggestions to your friend.

Ex. Let's eat lunch.   <u>おひるごはんを　食^たべましょう。</u>

1. Let's watch a movie.   _____

2. Let's speak Japanese.   _____

3. Let's study Japanese.   _____

D Using the situations below as cues, invite your friend to join you in the following activities.

Ex. Invite your friend to a movie on Saturday.

<u>土曜日に　いっしょに　えいがを　見^みませんか。</u>

1. Invite your friend to dinner at 6:30 on Friday.

_____

2. Invite your friend to listen to music together at around 8:00 p.m. on Friday.

_____

3. Invite your friend to do your Japanese homework together at around 3:30 p.m. on Sunday.

_____

E How should you respond in Japanese in the following situations?

1. You are busy and want to politely decline an invitation.

_____

2. You are happy to go (somewhere you've been invited to go to).

_____

Ⓐ <u>You are now AT SCHOOL</u>. Circle the correct verb from the choices given in the ( ), and then translate the sentences into English.

1. 今日　七時に　学校へ（行きました　来ました　かえりました）。

_____

2. 母は　きのう　ごぜん　九時ごろ　としょかんへ

（行きました　来ました　かえりました）。

_____

3. あには　きのうの　よる　十一時すぎに　うちへ

（行きました　来ました　かえりました）。

_____

4. 父は　今日　八時はんごろ　かいしゃへ

（行きました　来ました　かえりました）。

_____

Ⓑ Circle the correct particle from the choices given in the ( ), then translate the sentences into English.

1. 土曜日の　ごご　七時はんの　えいが（へ　に）　行きませんか。

_____

2. 父は　日曜日に　いつも　ゴルフ（へ　に）　行きます。

_____

3. ゆうがた　五時ごろ　としょかん（へ　に）　行きましょう。

_____

C What do you usually do after doing the first action? Fill in the blanks based on fact.

1. あさ　おきます。　それから、＿＿＿＿＿＿＿＿＿＿＿＿＿＿＿＿＿＿＿＿＿。

2. としょかんへ　行きます。　それから、＿＿＿＿＿＿＿＿＿＿＿＿＿＿＿＿。

D What time do you do these activities? Write the times using *hiragana*.

1. ＿＿＿＿＿＿＿＿＿＿＿＿＿＿　に　おきます。

2. ＿＿＿＿＿＿＿＿＿＿＿＿＿＿　に　あさごはんを　食べます。

3. ＿＿＿＿＿＿＿＿＿＿＿＿＿＿　に　学校へ　来ます。

4. ＿＿＿＿＿＿＿＿＿＿＿＿＿＿　に　おひるごはんを　食べます。

5. ＿＿＿＿＿＿＿＿＿＿＿＿＿＿　に　日本語の　クラスに　行きます。

6. ＿＿＿＿＿＿＿＿＿＿＿＿＿＿　に　うちへ　かえります。

7. ＿＿＿＿＿＿＿＿＿＿＿＿＿＿　に　ねます。

E Answer the questions based on fact.

1. きのうの　よる　何時に　ねましたか。

＿＿＿＿＿＿＿＿＿＿＿＿＿＿＿＿＿＿＿＿＿＿＿＿＿＿＿＿＿＿＿＿＿

2. 今日　何時に　おきましたか。

＿＿＿＿＿＿＿＿＿＿＿＿＿＿＿＿＿＿＿＿＿＿＿＿＿＿＿＿＿＿＿＿＿

3. 今日　何時に　学校へ　来ましたか。

＿＿＿＿＿＿＿＿＿＿＿＿＿＿＿＿＿＿＿＿＿＿＿＿＿＿＿＿＿＿＿＿＿

4. 今日　何時に　うちへ　かえりますか。

＿＿＿＿＿＿＿＿＿＿＿＿＿＿＿＿＿＿＿＿＿＿＿＿＿＿＿＿＿＿＿＿＿

A Fill in the blanks with appropriate vocabulary words based on the pictures, and fill in the circles with the appropriate particles.

1. _____ ◯ _____ ◯ _____ ◯ 行きました。

2. _____ ◯ _____ ◯ _____ ◯ 行きました。

3. _____ ◯ _____ ◯ _____ 行きます。

4. _____ ◯ _____ ◯ **library** ◯ 行きます。

older brother　　**high school**

5. _____ ◯ _____ ◯ _____ ◯ 行きます。

B Answer the questions below by filling in the (   ) with the appropriate response, then fill in the [   ] with the correct particle. Answer based on fact.

Ex. 何で　学校へ　来ますか。

（　じどうしゃ　）［　で　］来ます。

1. 何時に　学校へ　来ますか。

（　　　　　　　　　）［　　　］来ます。

2. だれと　学校へ　来ますか。

（　　　　　　　　　）［　　　］来ます。

3. 何時ごろに　うちへ　かえりますか。

（　　　　　　　　　）［　　　］かえります。

C Imagine that this was your schedule last Sunday. Using the cues given, complete the sentences with the correct times and particles.

Ex. 8:00 a.m.　　　　　　　　　　I got up.

（　ごぜん　八時に　　）おきました。

1. before 11:00 a.m.　　　　　　　I returned home.

（　　　　　　　　　）うちに　かえりました。

2. around 1:40 p.m.　　　　　　　My friend came to my house.

（　　　　　　　　　）ともだちは　うちに　来ました。

3. after 3:00 p.m.　　　　　　　　My friend and I went to a movie by car.

（　　　　　　　　　）ともだちと　えいがに　行きました。

4. around 6:30 p.m.　　　　　　　I returned home by bus.
　　　　　　　　　　　　　　　basu
（　　　　　　　　　）バスで　うちに　かえりました。

A Invite your friend to the following activities.

Ex. a party on Saturday

_土曜日に　パーティー^{paatii}に　行^いきませんか。_____

1. a meal on Friday

_____

2. shopping on Sunday

_____

3. a baseball game at 5:00 p.m. today

_____

4. a movie at 7:30 tonight

_____

B You have already suggested places to go with your friend. Now, suggest activities you can do at each location.

Ex. 山^{やま}へ　行^いきましょう。　そして、キャンプ^{kyanpu}を　しましょう。

1. うみへ　行^いきましょう。　そして、_____

2. デパート^{depaato}へ　行^いきましょう。

　　そして、_____

3. 日本の　レストラン^{resutoran}へ　行^いきましょう。

　　そして、_____

4. 日本へ　行^いきましょう。　そして、_____

C You were very sick and did not do anything yesterday. Respond using the appropriate words for "nothing" or "nowhere."

Ex. 何を　食べましたか。　　何も　食べませんでした。_____

1. 何を　のみましたか。　_____

2. 何を　しましたか。　_____

3. どこへ　行きましたか。　_____

D Your Japanese friend invites you to a party, but you have many questions.

a. Ask the following questions. Fill in each (　) with the correct question word and a particle if necessary.

1. When is the party?　　　　パーティーは　（　　　　　　　）ですか。

2. What time is the party?　　パーティーは　（　　　　　　　）ですか。

3. Where is the party?　　　　パーティーは　（　　　　　　　）ですか。

4. Who will come to the party?　パーティーに　（　　　　　）　来ますか。

5. What will you do at the party?　パーティーで　（　　　　　）　しますか。

b. Now write your Japanese friend's possible answers to the above questions.

1. パーティーは　（　　　　　　　　　　）です。

2. パーティーは　（　　　　　　　　　　）です。

3. パーティーは　（　　　　　　　　　　）です。

4. パーティーに　（　　　　　　　　　　　　　）　来ます。

5. パーティーで　（　　　　　　　　　　　　　）。

A Answer the questions using the English cues given.

Ex. いつ　りょ行を　しましたか。 (from December 15th to 20th)

　（　十二月十五日から　二十日まで　）　りょ行を　しました。

1. りょ行は　何曜日から　何曜日まででしたか。 (from Saturday to Friday)

　（　　　　　　　　　　　　　　　　　　　　）でした。

2. ひ行きは　何時から　何時まででしたか。 (from 2:10 a.m. to 10:35 p.m.)

　（　　　　　　　　　　　　　　　　　　　　）でした。

3. よく　あるきましたか。 (from morning till night)

　（　　　　　　　　　　　　　　　　　　　）あるきましたよ。

B Answer the questions in the past tense using the cues given in ( ).

Ex. 日本の　食べものは　どうでしたか。(好き)　好きでした。

1. お天きは　どうでしたか。(あつい) _____。

2. ひ行きは　どうでしたか。(ながい) _____。

3. ホテルは　どうでしたか。(いい) _____。
   _{hoteru}

4. とうきょうは　どうでしたか。(大好き) _____。

5. はな火は　どうでしたか。(きれい) _____。

6. かいものは　どうでしたか。(たかい) _____。

7. りょ行は　どうでしたか。(いそがしい) _____。

C You have invited your friend to travel with you to the places below. Suggest an activity you would like to do together there.

Ex. 日本へ　行^いきませんか。

そして、<u>おいしい　ものを　食^たべましょう</u>＿＿＿＿＿＿＿＿＿＿＿＿＿。

1. ハワイ^{hawai}へ　行^いきませんか。

そして、＿＿＿＿＿＿＿＿＿＿＿＿＿＿＿＿＿＿＿＿＿＿。

2. ディズニーランド^{dizuniirando}へ　行^いきませんか。

そして、＿＿＿＿＿＿＿＿＿＿＿＿＿＿＿＿＿＿＿＿＿＿。

よみましょう! Let's read!

Circle the correct answers based on the reading.

1. Who did not go on the Japan trip?
   a. the writer's father
   b. the writer's grandmother
   c. the writer's older sister
   d. the writer's younger sister

2. When did the writer travel?
   a. from Monday to Friday
   b. from Friday to Monday
   c. from Dec. 17 to 24
   d. from Dec. 18 to 23

3. Which statement is true?
   a. It was not cold.
   b. The flight was very long.
   c. The writer loved the Japanese pens.
   d. The writer saw lots of movies in Japan.

私は　おやすみに　日本へ　行きました。かぞく　四人と　りょ行しました。父と　母と　いもうとと　おばあさんと　いっしょに　行きました。十二月十八日、金曜日の　ひ行きでした。ひ行きは、とても　ながかったです。よく　えいがを　みました。日本は　とても　さむかったです。ラーメンが　おいしかったです。そして、たくさん　かいものを　しました。日本の　えんぴつが　だいすきでした。十二月二十三日の　水曜日に　かえりました。また　日本を　たのしみに　しています。

You may not know all the Japanese you hear, but use what you do know along with your imagination!

A You will listen once to a conversation between Ken and Emi. Choose the most appropriate answer to each question.

1. What time is it now?
- **a.** 9:00
- **b.** 9:17
- **c.** 9:30
- **d.** 9:37

2. What time does the Japanese class start?
- **a.** 9:00
- **b.** 9:17
- **c.** 9:30
- **d.** 9:37

B You will listen once to a conversation between Ken and Emi. Choose the most appropriate answer to each question.

1. Who invited a friend to see a movie?
- **a.** Emi
- **b.** Ken
- **c.** Ken's friend
- **d.** Emi's friend

2. What time is the movie?
- **a.** 3:45
- **b.** 4:00
- **c.** 4:15
- **d.** 4:30

3. What day of the week are they going to see the movie?
- **a.** Thursday
- **b.** Friday
- **c.** Saturday
- **d.** Sunday

4. What are they going to do after the movie?
- **a.** Have dinner at Ken's house.
- **b.** Have dinner at Emi's house.
- **c.** Have dinner at a restaurant.
- **d.** Have coffee at a coffee shop.

C You will listen once to a conversation between Ken and Emi. Choose the most appropriate answer to each question.

1. About what time is Emi going home?
- **a.** 3:30
- **b.** 4:00
- **c.** 4:15
- **d.** 4:30

2. About what time is Ken going home?
- **a.** 3:45
- **b.** 4:00
- **c.** 4:15
- **d.** 4:30

3. What are they going to do together? Choose two answers.
- **a.** going home
- **b.** shopping
- **c.** studying
- **d.** dining

4. Who suggested doing the activities mentioned in question 3?
- **a.** Ken
- **b.** Emi
- **c.** Ken's friend
- **d.** Emi's friend

D You will listen once to a conversation between Ken and Emi. Choose the most appropriate answer to each question.

1. What activities did Ken invite Emi to? Choose two answers.

   a. camping in the mountains

   b. picnic on the beach

   c. party at his house

   d. movie at his house

2. Which activity can Emi go to?

   a. Saturday's activity

   b. Sunday's activity

   c. both Saturday's and Sunday's activities

   d. neither Saturday's nor Sunday's activities

E You will listen once to a narrative. Choose the most appropriate answer to each question.

1. When was the speaker traveling?

   a. August 1–10

   b. August 2–8

   c. August 1–8

   d. August 2–10

2. Who did she travel with?

   a. friends

   b. siblings

   c. by herself

   d. parents

3. How does she describe the trip? Choose two answers.

   a. good

   b. hot

   c. expensive

   d. short

4. What is she looking forward to?

   a. traveling to another country

   b. traveling by ship next year

   c. traveling with her friends again

   d. traveling with her family next year

F You will listen once to a narrative. Choose the most appropriate answer to each question.

1. What does the speaker's mother do in the morning? Choose two answers.

   a. makes breakfast

   b. washes the dishes

   c. makes lunch

   d. goes to work

2. How does her father go to work?

   a. by car

   b. by train

   c. by bus

   d. by subway

3. Where does her sister go in the morning?

   a. middle school

   b. high school

   c. college

   d. company

4. What time does her brother get up?

   a. before 5:30 am

   b. before 6:00 am

   c. before 6:50 am

   d. before 7:10 am

A Circle the appropriate verb from the choices given.

1. ぼくの　犬^{いぬ}は　そとに　(A. あります　B. います)。

2. えんぴつけずりは　きょうしつに　(A. あります　B. います)。

3. きのう　母は　うちに　(A. あります　B. います　C. ありました

　D. いました)。

4. 今^{いま}　私^{わたし}は　学校^{がっこう}に　(A. あります　B. います　C. ありました

　D. いました)。

B The following items or people are either at your home or at school. Explain to your friend where the following people and things are, based on the following pictures.

Ex: own younger brother　おとうとは　学校^{がっこう}に　います。

1. pencil sharpener　＿＿＿＿＿＿＿＿＿＿＿＿＿＿＿＿＿＿＿＿＿＿＿＿＿＿＿＿＿

2. English teacher　＿＿＿＿＿＿＿＿＿＿＿＿＿＿＿＿＿＿＿＿＿＿＿＿＿＿＿＿＿

3. magazines　＿＿＿＿＿＿＿＿＿＿＿＿＿＿＿＿＿＿＿＿＿＿＿＿＿＿＿＿＿

4. cat　＿＿＿＿＿＿＿＿＿＿＿＿＿＿＿＿＿＿＿＿＿＿＿＿＿＿＿＿＿

5. telephone　＿＿＿＿＿＿＿＿＿＿＿＿＿＿＿＿＿＿＿＿＿＿＿＿＿＿＿＿＿

6. own mother　＿＿＿＿＿＿＿＿＿＿＿＿＿＿＿＿＿＿＿＿＿＿＿＿＿＿＿＿＿

C Mr. Tanaka visited Ms. Yamashita at her house. Complete the conversation between Mr. Tanaka and Ms. Yamashita using the English cues in the ( ).

田中: すみません。＿＿＿＿＿＿＿＿＿＿＿＿＿＿＿＿＿＿＿＿＿＿。

(Where is the trash can?)

山下: ごみばこですか。　ごみばこは ＿＿＿＿＿＿＿＿＿＿＿＿＿＿＿。

(is over there.)

田中: 犬は ＿＿＿＿＿＿＿＿＿＿＿＿＿＿＿＿＿＿＿＿＿＿＿＿＿＿＿。

(Where is your dog?)

山下: 犬ですか。　犬は ＿＿＿＿＿＿＿＿＿＿＿＿＿＿＿＿＿＿＿。

(was outside.)

今 そとに ＿＿＿＿＿＿＿＿＿＿＿＿＿＿＿＿＿＿＿＿＿。

(is not outside, right?)

田中: そうですね。

 よみましょう！ **Let's read!**

Circle the correct answers based on the reading.

1. Which statement is true about Ai (アイ)?
   a. Ai is a black dog.
   b. Ai is noisy.
   c. Ai mostly stays outside of the house.
   d. Ai does not like the writer's father.

2. Which statement is NOT true about Ai?
   a. Ai does not eat breakfast.
   b. Ai does not eat lunch.
   c. Ai does not eat dinner.
   d. Ai is a little chubby.

私の　うちの　犬の　名前は　アイ
です。三さいです。そして、アイは
しろいです。かわいいですが、うるさい
です。とても、げんきです。たいてい
うちに　いますが、ときどき　そとに
います。アイは　父が　だい好き
です。いつも　父と　いっしょに
います。アイは　あさごはんも　ひる
ごはんも　たべませんが、ちょっと
ふとっています。ばんごはんだけ
たべます。

名前 _____

日づけ _____ _____ 曜日

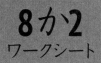

A Circle the correct response from the choices given. Ken and Emi are 15 and 16.

1. あの（女の子　男の子　女の人　男の人）は　ケンさんです。

2. あの（女の子　男の子　女の人　男の人）は　エミさんです。

3. あの（女の子　男の子　女の人　男の人）は　ケンさんの
お父さんです。

4. あの（女の子　男の子　女の人　男の人）は　ケンさんの
お母さんです。

5. あの（子ども　人　かた）は　ともだちの　おにいさんです。

6. あの　女の（子　人　かた）は　山本先生です。

B Based on the English cues, circle the best response from the choices given in the ( ).

Ex. ねこ（は　が）　うちに　（います　あります）。
(My cat is at my home.)

1. ともだちの　エミさん（は　が）　学校に　（いました　ありました）。
(My friend Emi was at school.)

2. あに（は　が）　かいしゃに　（います　あります）。
(My older brother is at the office.)

3. あそこに　プール（は　が）　（います　あります）よ。
(There is a pool over there.)

4. ここに　今日の　しゅくだい（は　が）　（います　あります）。
(Here is today's homework.)

C Answer the following questions in complete sentences based on the English cues given.

Ex. Q: プール^{puuru}に　だれが　いますか。　　　　　[Michiko and Akira]

　　A: みち子さんと　あきらさんが　います。

1. Q: きょうしつに　だれが　いますか。　　　　　[students]

　　A: _____

2. Q: そとに　何^{なに}が　いますか。　　　　　[a cute cat]

　　A: _____

3. Q: トイレ^{toire}は　どこに　ありますか。　　　　　[over there]

　　A: _____

4. Q: カフェテリア^{kafeteria}に　何^{なに}が　ありますか。　　　　　[food and drinks]

　　A: _____

D Text Chat

You will participate in a simulated exchange of text messages. You should respond as fully and as appropriately as possible.

You will have a conversation with a Japanese friend who invites you to go out this weekend.

1. こんにちは。　明日、　私の　うちに　来ませんか。

_____

2. 土曜日に　ともだちと　いっしょに　えいがに　行きましょうか。

_____

3. そして、　パーティー^{paatii}を　して、　十二時ごろに　かえりましょうか。

_____

4. 私^{わたし}は　たのしみに　して　います。

_____

A Match the items on the left with the correct counters on the right. Fill in the ( ) with the corresponding letter from the right column. *Hiragana* readings of the *kanji* are provided.

1. 木×3　　（　）

2. とり×2　　（　）

3. ぶた×8　　（　）

4. けしごむ×3　　（　）

5. 女の人×4　　（　）

6. 子ども×1　　（　）

7. あめ×5　　（　）

8. かみ×7　　（　）

9. ボールペン×9　　（　）

A. 四人

B. 一人

C. 七まい

D. 三本

E. 八ぴき

F. 三つ

G. 九本

H. 二わ

I. 五つ

B Complete the following sentences by writing the correct particles, or X if no particle, in the ( ). The meaning of each sentence pair is the same, but the emphasis is different.

Ex. one bird, tree

a. 木（に）　とり（が）　一わ（×）　います。　　[There is one bird in the tree.]

b. 一わ（の）　とり（が）　木（に）　います。　　[One bird is in the tree.]

1. two dogs, my house

a. うち（　）　いぬ（　）　二ひき（　）　います。　　[There are two dogs at home.]

b. 二ひき（　）　いぬ（　）　うち（　）　います。　　[Two dogs are at home.]

2. many flowers, over there

a. ここ（　）　はな（　）　たくさん（　）　あります。　[There are many flowers here.]

b. たくさん（　）　はな（　）　ここ（　）　あります。　[Many flowers are here.]

C Write a sentence describing the location and amount of each item, based on the English cues given. Write in complete sentences using the appropriate particles and counters.

Ex. classroom, ten children　　<u>きょうしつに　子<ruby>こ</ruby>どもが　十<ruby>にん</ruby>人　います。</u>

1. outside, one cat　　_____-_____

2. my house, two cars　　_____-_____

3. here, many pencils　　_____-_____

4. pond, ten fish　　_____-_____

よみましょう!　Let's read!

私は　<u>中村<ruby>なかむら</ruby>はる子<ruby>こ</ruby></u>です。　<u>三<ruby>み</ruby>たか高校<ruby>こうこう</ruby></u>の　一年生<ruby>ねんせい</ruby>です。

かぞくは　父と　母と　二人<ruby>ふたり</ruby>の　いもうとが　います。　私<ruby>わたし</ruby>は

ねこが　大好<ruby>だいす</ruby>きです。　うちに　ねこが　五ひき　います。　でも、

犬<ruby>いぬ</ruby>は　いません。　そして、　さかなが　十ぴき　います。　うちの

にわ*は　とても　小<ruby>ちい</ruby>さいですが、　にわに　たくさんの　はなが

あります。　母も　私<ruby>わたし</ruby>も　はなが　大好<ruby>だいす</ruby>きです。　(*にわ: a garden)

Circle the correct answers based on the reading.

1. How many and what kind of pets does Haruko have?
   a. five cats, one dog, nine fish
   b. four cats, no dog, ten fish
   c. five cats, one dog, ten fish
   d. five cats, no dog, ten fish

2. Which statement is NOT true?
   a. The garden is spacious.
   b. There are many flowers in the garden.
   c. Haruko loves flowers.
   d. Haruko's mother loves flowers.

名前 _____

日づけ _____ _____ 曜日

(A) Answer the following questions about your school.

Ex. 学校は　ふるいですか。　　　いいえ、ふるくないです。

1. 学校は　ゆうめいですか。　_____

2. 学校は　大きいですか。　_____

3. きょうしつは　きれいですか。　_____

4. たてものは　あたらしいですか。　_____

5. みどりが　うつくしいですか。　_____

(B) Describe the following things and people in two separate sentences, using appropriate descriptive words.

Ex. すもうとり sumo wrestler

からだが　大きいです。_____　太っています。_____

1. 学校の　プール *puuru*

_____

2. 学校の　ロッカー *rokkaa*

_____

3. あなたの　お母さん

_____

4. 日本語の　先生

_____

C What do you say when you want to know where the following places and people are? Complete the questions by writing the English cue in Japanese, then circle the correct verb from the choices given.

1. (bathroom)

_____は、　どこに（あります　います）か。

2. (school office)

_____は、　どこに（あります　います）か。

3. (your friend Daisuke)

_____は、　どこに（あります　います）か。

D Text Chat: You will participate in a simulated exchange of text messages. You should respond as fully and as appropriately as possible.

You will have a conversation with a new Japanese exchange student, who has a few questions about your Japanese class.

1. はじめまして。　山田えみ子です。　どうぞ　よろしく。

_____

2. 日本語の　きょうしつに　生徒が　何人　いますか。

_____

3. 日本語が　好きですか。

_____

4. 日本語の　しゅくだいが　たくさん　ありますか。

_____

5. ありがとう。　また　チャット　しましょう。

_____

A Circle the correct response, based on fact.

1. 日本語の　きょうしつは　（ひろい　せまい）です。

2. 日本語の　きょうしつの　たてものは　（あたらしい　ふるい）です。

3. 日本語の　きょうしつに　生徒が　（たくさん　すこし）います。

4. 日本語の　先生は　（男　女）の　先生です。

5. トイレは　（とおい　ちかい）です。

B Answer the questions about your house using complete sentences.

1. うちは　大きいですか。 _____

2. うつくしい　にわが　ありますか。 _____

3. うちに　車が　何だい　ありますか。 _____

4. うちは　何いろですか。 _____

5. うちは　あたらしいですか。 _____

C Answer the questions about your room using complete sentences.

1. へやは　ひろいですか。 _____

2. へやは　きれいですか。 _____

3. つくえと　いすが　ありますか。 _____

4. 大きい　ベッドが　ありますか。 _____

5. ごきぶりが　いますか。 _____

D Write the appropriate antonym (opposite) for each word below, and give the English definition of the antonym.

Ex. 大（おお）きい　　小（ちい）さい　　　small

1. ひろい　　　_____

2. きれい　　　_____

3. とおい　　　_____

4. せが　たかい　_____

5. ながい　　　_____

6. 好（す）き　　　_____

7. とくい　　　_____

8. 太（ふと）って　います　_____

9. 年（とし）を　とって　います　_____

10. しずか　　　_____

11. ふるい　　　_____

12. たくさん　　_____

13. きびしい　　_____

14. わるい　　　_____

15. 上手（じょうず）　　_____

よみましょう!　Let's read!

Circle the correct answers based on the reading.

1. Which statement is NOT true about the writer?
   a. The writer is a girl.
   b. The writer is twelve years old.
   c. The writer has one younger brother.
   d. The writer is not very healthy.

2. Which statement is true about the writer?
   a. The writer's room is spacious.
   b. The writer enjoys the trees outside her window.
   c. The writer sees a red bird every morning.
   d. The writer enjoys talking to a yellow bird.

私は　十二さいの　女の子です。あにが　一人　います。父も　母も　あにも　げんきですが、私は　あまり　げんきでは　ありません。私の　へやは　とても　せまいですが、まどの　そとに木が　あります。そして、あさ　きいろい　とりが　まいにち　来ます。私は　とりと　はなします。この　とりが　大好きです。

You may not know all the Japanese you hear, but use what you do know along with your imagination!

A **You will listen once to a conversation between Ken and Emi. Choose the most appropriate answer to each question.**

1. What color are the flowers?

  a. red

  b. yellow

  c. purple

  d. blue

2. What color are the birds?

  a. red

  b. yellow

  c. purple

  d. blue

3. How many birds are there?

  a. one

  b. two

  c. three

  d. four

4. How many fish are in the pond?

  a. one

  b. six

  c. eight

  d. ten

5. How many tall trees are there?

  a. one

  b. two

  c. three

  d. four

B **You will listen once to a conversation between Ken and Emi. Choose the most appropriate answer to each question.**

1. Who is at the hospital? Choose two answers.

  a. Emi's father

  b. Emi's mother

  c. Emi's grandfather

  d. Emi's grandmother

2. Where is Emi's younger brother?

  a. at the hospital

  b. at the beach

  c. in the mountains

  d. at home

3. Who went to the beach?

  a. Emi's father

  b. Emi's mother

  c. Emi's sister

  d. Emi's brother

4. Who did Ken meet for the first time?

  a. Emi's father

  b. Emi's mother

  c. Emi's older brother

  d. Emi's grandfather

C You will listen once to a narrative. Choose the most appropriate answer to each question.

1. What is the speaker's grade level?
   a. 9th
   b. 10th
   c. 11th
   d. 12th

2. Where does he live? Choose two answers.
   a. in Tokyo
   b. in Kyoto
   c. near his school
   d. far from his school

3. Which description is NOT true about the speaker's school?
   a. The school is beautiful.
   b. The school is not very spacious.
   c. There is a pond on the school grounds.
   d. There is a large pool on the campus.

4. What is not in his classroom?
   a. trash can
   b. window
   c. pencil sharpener
   d. desk

5. How many female students are in his class?
   a. 14
   b. 17
   c. 23
   d. 40

6. What is his opinion of his school?
   a. It is strict and difficult.
   b. It is old and dirty.
   c. It is famous and good.
   d. It is new and small.

D You will listen once to a narrative. Choose the most appropriate answer to each question.

1. Where is the speaker's house?
   a. near the beach
   b. near the mountains
   c. far from her school
   d. near a river

2. How many rooms are there in her house?
   a. two
   b. three
   c. four
   d. five

3. What item is not in her room?
   a. desk
   b. trash can
   c. computer
   d. pencil sharpener

4. What is by the door?
   a. a small window
   b. a big window
   c. a small chair
   d. a big chair

5. Which color fish is not in the pond?
   a. black
   b. white
   c. gold
   d. red

6. How many cats does she have?
   a. one
   b. two
   c. three
   d. four

Ⓐ **Fill in the blanks based on Mary's class schedule below. It is now <u>seven o'clock in the evening on Wednesday 2/27</u>.**

Time	2/27 Wed. (**Today**)	2/28 Thu.	2/29 Fri.
8:10 — 8:20 a.m.	Homeroom	Homeroom	Homeroom
8:30 — 9:30 a.m.	Japanese (HW*)	Japanese (HW*)	Japanese (Exam)
9:45 — 10:45 a.m.	Math (HW*)	Math (HW*)	Math (HW*)
11:00 — 12:00 a.m.	Music	Art	Music
12:00 — 1:30 p.m.	Lunch break	Lunch break	Lunch break
1:30 — 3:30 p.m.	Social Studies	Science (HW*)	Physical Education

* HW = homework

1. ホームルームは 毎日 何時から 何時まで ありますか。

 （　　　　　）から （　　　　　）まで あります。

2. おひるの 休み時かんは いつですか。

 （　　　　　）から （　　　　　）までです。

3. 今日 何の しゅくだいが ありましたか。

 （　　　）と （　　　）の しゅくだいが ありました。

4. 明日 何の じゅぎょうが ありますか。

 （　　　）と （　　　）と（　　　）と （　　　）です。

5. 日本語の しけんは いつですか。

 （　）月（　　　）日（　　）曜日の （　　　　　）です。
　　　　　　　　　　　　　　　　　　　　　　time

B Write your schedule for today. Include your breaks and your after school activities.

～から　～まで		かもく	English
Ex. 8時30分から　9時10分まで		日本語	Japanese

C Answer the following questions based on fact. Use complete sentences.

1. 何_{なん}の　かもくが　好きですか。 _____

2. 何_{なん}の　かもくが　にが手ですか。 _____

3. 毎_{まい}日　日本語_ごの　しゅくだいが　ありますか。 _____

D カタカナのれんしゅう: Write the English equivalent of the following universities.

1. スタンフォード _____

2. プリンストン _____

3. ブラウン _____

4. アラバマ _____

5. ハーバード _____

6. イェール _____

7. ラトガーズ _____

8. ノースウェスターン _____

9. バークレー _____

10. コロラドボルダー _____

名前 _____

日づけ _____ _____ 曜日

A Complete the following sentences by filling in appropriate information based on your opinion. Choose そして or でも based on the context. Translate each sentence into English.

Ex. 先生は　<u>きびしいです</u>。　(そして　(でも))、<u>とても　いいです</u>。

English: <u>My teacher is strict. However, he is very good.</u>

1. 英語の　じゅぎょうは_____。　(そして　でも)、_____。

English: _____

2. 日本語の　つぎの　じゅぎょうは_____。　(そして　でも)、_____。

English: _____

3. 日本語の　しゅくだいは_____。　(そして　でも)、_____。

English: _____

4. たいいくの　先生は_____。　(そして　でも)、_____。

English: _____

5. おひるの　休み時かんは_____。　(そして　でも)、_____。

English: _____

6. ともだちは_____。　(そして　でも)、_____。

English: _____

7. 学校は_____。　(そして　でも)、_____。

English: _____

B Answer the following questions based on fact.

1. 数学の　じゅぎょうは　何時から　何時までですか。

_____

2. 先生は　だれですか。

_____

3. どんな　先生ですか。

_____

4. じゅぎょうは　どうですか。

_____

5. 毎日　数学の　しゅくだいが　ありますか。

_____

C カタカナのれんしゅう

a. Write the following words in *katakana*.

1. door _____   5. Jon _____

2. juice _____   6. France _____

3. restaurant _____   7. Germany _____

4. department store _____   8. engineer _____

b. Write the English equivalent of the following *katakana* words.

1. フロリダ _____   5. ヴァージニア _____

2. コネチカット _____   6. ワシントン _____

3. カリフォルニア _____   7. テキサス _____

4. ニューヨーク _____   8. ミシガン _____

A Match the appropriate reasons and results by writing the correct letter from the right column in the ( ).

<u>Reasons</u>

<u>Results</u>

( ) 1. 学校は　とおくないです。

A. 水えいに　行きましょう。

( ) 2. あついです。

B. パーティーを　します。

( ) 3. 金曜日は　私の　たんじょう日です。

C. うれしいです。

( ) 4. せいせきが　ひどいです。

D. あるいて　行きます。

( ) 5. しけんが　良かったです。

E. かなしいです。

B Connect the reasons and results above into one sentence using から、 then translate the sentences into English. Be sure to write the reason <u>first</u>!

1. _____。

英語:_____

2. _____。

英語:_____

3. _____。

英語:_____

4. _____。

英語:_____

5. _____。

英語:_____

C Answer the following questions negatively.

1. 今日は　あついですか。　　　　　いいえ、＿＿＿＿＿＿＿＿＿＿＿＿

2. きのうは　あつかったですか。　　いいえ、＿＿＿＿＿＿＿＿＿＿＿＿

3. としょかんは　しずかですか。　　いいえ、＿＿＿＿＿＿＿＿＿＿＿＿

4. まえ　日本語が　上手でしたか。　いいえ、＿＿＿＿＿＿＿＿＿＿＿＿

5. ベンさんは　あたまが　いいですか。いいえ、＿＿＿＿＿＿＿＿＿＿＿

6. しけんは　良かったですか。　　　いいえ、＿＿＿＿＿＿＿＿＿＿＿＿

7. 数学の　しけんは　明日ですか。　いいえ、＿＿＿＿＿＿＿＿＿＿＿＿

8. パーティーは　土曜日でしたか。　いいえ、＿＿＿＿＿＿＿＿＿＿＿＿

D Answer the questions, then translate your answers into English.

Ex. しつもん：　なぜ　しゃかいの　せいせきが　わるかったですか。

こたえ：　<u>べんきょうしませんでしたから。</u>

英語：　<u>Because I did not study . . .</u>

1. しつもん：　なぜ　うれしいですか。

こたえ：　＿＿＿＿＿＿＿＿＿＿＿＿＿＿＿＿＿＿＿＿＿

英語：　＿＿＿＿＿＿＿＿＿＿＿＿＿＿＿＿＿＿＿＿＿

2. しつもん：　なぜ　学校が　好きですか。

こたえ：　＿＿＿＿＿＿＿＿＿＿＿＿＿＿＿＿＿＿＿＿＿

英語：　＿＿＿＿＿＿＿＿＿＿＿＿＿＿＿＿＿＿＿＿＿

A Circle the correct particle from the choices given, then circle whether you want or do not want the things listed below.

1. お金（は　が）　（ほしい　ほしくない）です。

2. しけん（は　が）　（ほしい　ほしくない）です。

3. 車（は　が）　（ほしい　ほしくない）です。

4. しゅくだい（は　が）　（ほしい　ほしくない）です。

B Circle the correct particle and word from the choices given in the ( ) to indicate whether there is a lot or a few of something based on your opinion.

1. 日本語は　しゅくだい（は　が）　（おおい　すくない）です。

2. 休み（は　が）　（おおい　おおくない）です。

3. 英語の　しゅくだい（は　が）　（おおい　すくない）です。

4. ぼくは　ともだち（は　が）　（すくない　すくなくない）です。

C Complete the following sentences by changing the words in the ( ) into the <u>past</u> tense.

1. 日本の　なつは　とても _____（あつい）。

2. いい　せいせきが _____（ほしい）。

3. 今しゅう　しゅくだいは _____（おおくない）。

4. しけんは _____（やさしくない）。

D Text Chat

You will participate in a simulated exchange of text messages. Respond as fully and as appropriately as possible. You will have a conversation with your Japanese friend.

1. こんにちは。　おげんきですか。

_____

2. しゅうまつは　たのしかったですか。　何_{なに}を　しましたか。

_____

3. 日本語_ごの　べんきょうは　たいへんですか。　なぜですか。

_____

4. 先_{せん}しゅうの　日本語_ごの　テストは　良_よかったですか。

_____

5. この　しゅうまつに　何_{なに}を　しますか。(Name two activities.)

_____

6. 私に　しつもんが　ありますか。　では、おげんきで。

_____

E カタカナをよみましょう。 Write the English equivalent of the following *katakana* words.

1. バイオリン _____
4. クラリネット _____

2. フルート _____
5. トランペット _____

3. ドラム _____
6. ヴィオラ _____

Ⓐ **Fill in the underlined spaces with the correct dates, and write the *hiragana* readings of the underlined portion.**

*NOTE: Start off years with thousand (せん) or two thousand (にせん).

Ex. 母の　たんじょう日は　<u>1970年^{ねん}</u>　<u>1月</u>　<u>30日</u>です。

　　*（せんきゅうひゃくななじゅうねん　いちがつ　さんじゅうにち）

1. 私の　たんじょう日は　_____ 年^{ねん}　____ 月　____ 日です。

　（　　　　　　　　　　　　　　　　　　　　　　　　　　　）

2. 今年^{ことし}は　_____ 年^{ねん}です。

　（　　　　　　　　　　　　　　　　　　　　　　　　　　　）

3. きょ年^{ねん}は　_____ 年^{ねん}でした。

　（　　　　　　　　　　　　　　　　　　　　　　　　　　　）

Ⓑ **Answer the questions using the 〜や　〜など pattern.**

Ex. 日本語^ごの　きょうしつに　何^{なに}が　ありますか。

　<u>つくえや　いすなど（が）　あります。</u>

1. 何^{なん}の　食^たべものが　好きですか。

　_____

2. 今日^{きょう}、　何^{なん}の　じゅぎょうが　ありますか。

　_____

3. クリスマスに　何^{なに}が　ほしいですか。

　_____

C Answer the following questions based on fact.

Ex. 土曜日に　しゅくだいを　しますか。　　<u>いいえ、　しません。</u>

1. ほうかごに　何_{なに}を　しますか。　　_____

1. ほうかごに　何を　しますか。 — (reading: なに over 何)

2. しゅうまつに　だれと　あそびますか。　_____

3. しゅうまつに　およぎますか。　　_____

4. 毎_{まい}日　うたいますか。　　_____

5. テレビゲームが　好きですか。　　_____

6. 来年_{らいねん}も　日本語_ごを　べんきょうしますか。_____

よみましょう! **Let's read!**

Circle the correct answers based on the reading.

1. Which statement is true?
 a. There is a math exam every week.
 b. The math exams are sometimes easy.
 c. There is not much math homework.
 d. The writer is good at math.

2. Which statement is true?
 a. The writer's math exam last week was good.
 b. The writer's math class is one hour long.
 c. The writer's math teacher is strict.
 d. The writer thinks math is too hard for her.

3. Which statement is true?
 a. The writer likes to study.
 b. The writer does not like school.
 c. The writer enjoys after school activities.
 d. The writer thinks her school life is boring.

私は　がっこうが　好きですが、べんきょうは　とくいでは　ありません。先しゅうの　すうがくの　しけんは　ひどかったです。かなしいですが、私は　すうがくが　分かりません。じゅぎょうは、九時はんから　十一時までです。先生は　やさしいんですが、しゅくだいが　おおいです。それに、毎しゅう　しけんが　ありますから、たいへんです。ほうかご、私は　バンドの　れんしゅうや　ダンスの　レッスンが　ありますから、毎日　とても　いそがしいですが、たのしいです。

You may not know all the Japanese you hear, but use what you do know along with your imagination!

A You will listen once to a conversation between Ken and Emi. Choose the most appropriate answer to each question.

1. Which class is Emi going to have next?
   a. P.E.
   b. music
   c. math
   d. science

2. How does Emi describe her teacher?
   a. strict and difficult
   b. strict but good
   c. interesting and good
   d. interesting but difficult

3. How does Emi describe her class?
   a. difficult and boring
   b. easy but boring
   c. interesting and fun
   d. interesting but difficult

4. What time does the class start?
   a. 8:50
   b. 9:00
   c. 9:10
   d. 9:15

B You will listen once to a narrative. Choose the most appropriate answer to each question.

1. When did the speaker take the exam?
   a. last week
   b. this morning
   c. the day before yesterday
   d. yesterday

2. What were the results of the exam?
   a. He did not study so he received a bad grade.
   b. Despite studying, he received a bad grade.
   c. Despite not studying, he received a good grade.
   d. He prepared for the test, so he received a good grade.

3. What is his opinion of the class?
   a. It is boring and hard.
   b. It is interesting, but difficult.
   c. It is interesting and easy.
   d. It is boring and easy.

4. Which description matches his teacher?
   a. an older male teacher
   b. a young male teacher
   c. a young female teacher
   d. an older female teacher

5. How does he describe his teacher?
   a. boring and easy
   b. interesting but strict
   c. interesting and fun
   d. boring and strict

6. What is he going to do this weekend?
   a. He will study for a good grade.
   b. He has to study to make up his work.
   c. He is not going to study, but have fun.
   d. He does not have to study because he has good grades.

C You will listen once to a narrative. Choose the most appropriate answer to each question.

1. What kind of day is the speaker having?
   a. busy
   b. easy
   c. fun
   d. interesting

2. Which class starts from 8:15?
   a. social studies
   b. science
   c. math
   d. English

3. Which class ends at 3:30?
   a. math
   b. science
   c. music
   d. art

4. How many breaks does she have?
   a. one
   b. two
   c. three
   d. none

D You will listen once to a conversation between Ken and Emi. Choose the most appropriate answer to each question.

1. How is Emi?
   a. She is disappointed.
   b. She is sad.
   c. She is happy.
   d. She is busy.

2. What did Emi do recently?
   a. She took a math exam last week.
   b. She took a science exam last week.
   c. She took a math exam the day before yesterday.
   d. She took a science exam the day before yesterday.

3. How was Emi's exam?
   a. easy
   b. difficult
   c. long
   d. short

4. How did Ken do on his exam?
   a. He earned a good grade on his test because he studied.
   b. He did terribly on the exam because he did not study.
   c. Even though he did not study, he earned a good grade.
   d. Even though he studied, he did not do well on the exam.

E You will listen once to a conversation between Ken and Emi. Choose the most appropriate answer to each question.

1. What is Emi going to do after school?
   a. sports and music
   b. shopping and studying
   c. sports and studying
   d. music and studying

2. What is Emi looking forward to?
   a. traveling this year
   b. spending time with her friends
   c. traveling with her family
   d. traveling next year

Ⓐ Ken is having many problems and is in pain. He is at his doctor's office. Help him explain his problems to his doctor.

いしゃ: どう しましたか。

ケン: 1.( ) が いたい(ん)です。

2.( ) が たかい(ん)です。

3.( ) が いたい(ん)です。

4.( ) が いたい(ん)です。

5.( ) が いたい(ん)です。

6.( ) が しにました。

7.( ) が わるかった(ん)です。

8.( ) が びょうきです。

いしゃ: そうですか。 では、おだいじに。

Ⓑ Circle the correct response from the choices given.

1. 先生: どう しましたか。

   生徒: *母が* びょうきです。

   先生: (a. おだいじに。 b. かわいそうに。 c. ざんねんですねえ。)

2. 先生: どう しましたか。

   生徒: 私の ねこが しにました。

   先生: (a. おだいじに。 b. かわいそうに。 c. ざんねんでしたねえ。)

C The following is a conversation between a teacher and a student. Complete the conversation using the English cues given.

先生： どう　しましたか。

生徒： ＿＿＿＿＿＿＿＿＿＿＿＿＿＿＿＿＿＿＿＿＿＿＿＿＿＿＿。
(I am sad.)

先生： なぜですか。

生徒： ＿＿＿＿＿＿＿＿＿＿＿＿＿＿＿＿＿＿＿＿＿＿＿＿＿＿＿。
(My test today was terrible.)

先生： ＿＿＿＿＿＿＿＿＿＿＿＿＿＿＿＿＿＿＿＿＿＿＿＿＿＿＿。
(Did you study?)

生徒： いいえ、＿＿＿＿＿＿＿＿＿＿＿＿＿＿＿＿＿＿＿＿＿、
(Because I went to a dance (party) last night,)

ぜんぜん　べんきょうしませんでした。

先生： だめですよ。

 よみましょう!　**Let's read!**

Circle the correct answers based on the reading.

1. What happened to the writer?
   a. The writer had a stomach ache.
   b. The writer lost a dog.
   c. The writer had a bad cold.
   d. The writer had a sore throat.

2. How was the writer's appetite?
   a. The writer drank water in the morning.
   b. The writer ate a little in the morning.
   c. The writer did not want any drink at night.
   d. The writer could eat a lot at night.

きのうは　日曜日でしたが、たいへんでした。私は　あさ　ねつが　とても　たかかったんです。あたまも　とても　いたかったんです。たべものは　なにも　ほしくなかったんです。のみものも　あまり　ほしくなかったです。お水は　のみました。私は　母と　びょういんへ行きました。とても　わるい　かぜでした。うちで　よく　ねました。そして、よるは　だいじょうぶでした。ばんごはんは　すこし　たべました。

A Read each of the conversations, then circle the correct response from the choices given.

Ex. エミ: 今　テニスを(or が)　したいですか。

ケン: いいえ、テニス　(を　が　(は))　((したくない)　したくなかった)
　　　です。

1. エミ: 今日　うちへ　(早い　早く)　かえりたいですか。

ケン: いいえ、(早い　早く)　(かえりたくない　かえりたくなかった)
　　　です。

2. エミ: ゆうべ　テレビを(or が)　見たかったですか。

ケン: いいえ、テレビ(を　が　は)　(見たくない　見たくなかった)
　　　です。

3. エミ: びょうきですか。　明日　学校(を　から)　休みますか。

ケン: だいじょうぶですよ。　ぼくは　学校(を　から　は)

　　　(休みたくない　休みたくなかった)　です。

B Answer the questions **negatively**.

Ex. 今　ねむいですか。　　　　　いいえ、ねむくないです。

1. 今　休みたいですか。　　　　いいえ、_____。

2. あたまが　いたい(ん)ですか。　いいえ、_____。

3. ねつが　たかかった(ん)ですか。　いいえ、_____。

4. 大学へ　行きたかった(ん)ですか。いいえ、_____。

C Complete each sentence using the pattern of "want to do" or "wanted to do".

Ex. ゆうべ　つかれていましたから、　早^{はや}く　<u>ねたかったです。</u>

1. あたまが　いたい(です)から、　くすりを　_____。

2. 明日　しけんが　ありますから、　今晩^{ばん}　_____。

3. ゆうべ　おそく　ねましたから、　今晩^{ばん}　早^{はや}く　_____。

4. ひどい　かぜですから、今日　学校^{がっこう}を　_____。

D カタカナをかきましょう。

1. cake (*keeki*) _____   5. aspirin (*asupirin*) _____

2. gum (*gamu*) _____   6. toast (*toosuto*) _____

3. milk (*miruku*) _____   7. juice (*juusu*) _____

4. cola (*koora*) _____   8. fruits (*furuutsu*) _____

E Based on the following situations, choose the correct answer.

1. You brought cookies to your class. Offer some to your teacher.

　a. クッキーが　ほしいですか。

　b. クッキーを　食^たべたいですか。

　c. クッキーを　どうぞ。

2. Your teacher said her/his mother passed away. What do you say to your teacher?

　a. かわいそうに。

　b. おきのどくに。

　c. お大^{だい}じに。

名前 _____

日づけ _____ _____ 曜日

A Write the English meaning of each adjective in the (   ) and write the adjective's antonym (opposite) in the blank.

Ex. あたらしい　(new)_____ふるい_____

1. ひくい　(　　　　　)_____
2. あつい　(　　　　　)_____
3. くろい　(　　　　　)_____
4. とおい　(　　　　　)_____
5. つよい　(　　　　　)_____
6. ひろい　(　　　　　)_____
7. きらい　(　　　　　)_____
8. わるい　(　　　　　)_____

9. 早_{はや}い　(　　　　　)_____
10. しずか　(　　　　　)_____
11. きれい　(　　　　　)_____
12. 大_{おお}きい　(　　　　　)_____
13. むずかしい　(　　　　　)_____
14. みじかい　(　　　　　)_____
15. きびしい　(　　　　　)_____

B Using the adjectives above, describe the following pictures with an adjective and noun.

Ex. 　　　1. 　　　2. 　　　3. 　　　4.

Ex. わるい　せいせきです。

1. (　　　　　　　　　　)です。　　3. (　　　　　　　　　　)です。

2. (　　　　　　　　　　)です。　　4. (　　　　　　　　　　)です。

よみましょう! Let's read!

　　ぼくたちは　ゆうべ　バスケットの　しあいを　見ました。

しあいは　ごご　八時はんからでした。　マッキンレー高校と

ルーズベルト高校の　しあいでした。　マッキンレー高校は

かちました。　マッキンレー高校の　チームは　とても

つよかったです。　マッキンレー高校の　チームは　みなさん

せが　とても　高かったです。

　　ぼくは　ゆうべ　おそく　うちへ　かえりました。　よる

十一時すぎでした。　しあいは　おもしろかったんですが、　ぼくは

とても　つかれて　いました。　今朝　ぼくは　のどが

いたかったです。　そして、　ねつも　すこし　ありましたから、

学校を　休みました。　今　すこし　げんきです。　明日は

学校へ　行きます。

Circle the correct answers based on the reading.

1. What time did the game start?
   a. 8:30 a.m.
   b. 9:30 a.m.
   c. 8:30 p.m.
   d. 9:30 p.m.

2. Which statement is true?
   a. Roosevelt High School lost.
   b. McKinley High School lost.
   c. The McKinley players were short.
   d. The game was not fun.

3. Why was the writer tired last night?
   a. He/she returned home from the game very late.
   b. He/she played throughout the game.
   c. He/she watched the whole game at home.
   d. He/she went to the movie after the game.

4. Which statement about the writer is correct?
   a. He/she went to school today.
   b. He/she will be absent from school tomorrow.
   c. He/she had a high fever today.
   d. He/she feels a little better now.

A Circle the correct particle from the choices given.

1. きれい（X　な　の）　はなですねえ。

2. 父の　好き（X　な　の）　食べものは　おすしです。

3. ゆうべ　とても　おもしろい（X　な　の）　えいがを　見ました。

4. 来しゅうの　金曜日に　大じ（X　な　の）　しあいが　あります。

5. 田中先生は　きびしい（X　な　の）　先生です。

B Fill in the blank with the adjective indicated in the ( ) and include a particle if necessary.

Ex. うたが　__上手な__　生徒ですねえ。 (skillful)

1. 私は　_____　はなが　好きです。 (red)

2. マリさんは　とても　_____　女の子です。 (cute)

3. まりさんの　おねえさんは　とても　_____　人です。 (pretty)

4. ともだちは　とても　_____　人です。 (important)

5. おとうとは　とても　_____　子どもです。 (noisy)

6. ぼくたちは　とても　_____　チームです。 (weak)

7. _____　食べものは　何ですか。 (dislike)

8. 日本語の　しけんは　_____　せいせきでした。 (terrible)

C Write the *hiragana* reading of the underlined *kanji* in the (   ), and complete the sentence by writing the correct word in *kanji* in the blank and the *hiragana* reading in the (   ).

Ex. 今日 (きょう)は　火曜日 (かようび)です。

1. 先月 (   )は　四月 (   )でした。

   今月 (   )は　_____ (   )です。

2. 今月は　七月 (   )です。_____ (   )は

   八月です。

3. 日本の　なつは　あついですが、_____は　さむいです。

4. はるに　イースターが　あります。　そして、_____に

   サンクスギビングが　あります。

D Write the letter of the correct response from the box below for each of the following situations.

1. 日本語の　しけんの　せいせきは　Fでした。　____

2. 明日　大じな　しあいが　あります。　____

3. おなかが　いたいです。　____

---

a. いいですねえ。　　b. ざんねんですねえ。　　c. ざんねんでしたねえ。

d. かわいそうに。　　e. だいじょうぶですか。　　f. がんばって。

E カタカナをかきましょう。

1. hot dog (*hottodoggu*) _____

2. cookie (*kukkii*) _____

3. ice cream (*aisukuriimu*) _____

4. popcorn (*poppukoon*) _____

5. sneakers (*suniikaa*) _____

6. pants (*pantsu*) _____

7. jacket (*jaketto*) _____

8. T-shirt (*tiishatsu*) _____

A Circle the correct particle and answer the questions using the English cues.

Ex. バスケットの　しあいは　どこ（（で）　に）　ありますか。[Washington High]

　　しあいは、　<u>ワシントン高校で　あります。</u>

1. 田中さんは　どこ（で　に）　いますか。　　　　　[Japanese classroom]

　　田中さんは、_____。

2. 水えいの　れんしゅうは　どこ（で　に）　ありますか。[school pool]

　　れんしゅうは、_____。

3. たいてい　どこ（で　に）　本を　よみますか。　　[library]

　　本は　たいてい　_____。

4. 何時に　どこ（で　に）　あいましょうか。　　　　[my house]

　　五時に　_____。

5. 今朝　何（で　に）　学校へ　来ましたか。　　　　[bicycle]

　　今朝　学校へ　_____。

6. 今晩の　えいがは　どこ（で　に）　ありますか。[university]

　　えいがは　_____。

7. 学校の　まえ（で　に）　はしりますか。　　　　　[after]

　　いいえ、_____。

B テキストチャット

You will participate in a simulated exchange of text messages. You should respond as fully and as appropriately as possible.

You will have a conversation with Mari, a Japanese student that you met at school, and who has now returned to Japan.

1. まり: こんにちは。 おげんきですか。
    Start the conversation.

_____

2. まり: 私は 今 あまり げんきでは ありません。 かぜです。
    Show your sympathy. Ask about a specific symptom.

_____

3. まり: 私は 大じょうぶです。 でも、 学校を 二日 休みました。
    Respond.

_____

4. まり: 毎日 ほうかごで 何を しますか。 何時ごろ うちに
    かえりますか。
    Respond.

_____

5. まり: そうですか。 スポーツの しあいに 行きますか。 どの
    スポーツチームは つよいですか。
    State your opinion.

_____

6. まり: この チャットは たのしかったです。 また しましょう。
    End the conversation.

_____

You may not know all the Japanese you hear, but use what you do know along with your imagination!

A **You will listen once to a conversation between Ken and Emi. Choose the most appropriate answer to each question.**

1. What happened to Emi?
   a. She caught a cold.
   b. Her dog died.
   c. She lost her game.
   d. She did not do well on her test.

2. What happened to Ken?
   a. He caught a cold.
   b. His dog died.
   c. He lost his game.
   d. He did not do well on his test.

B **You will listen once to a conversation between Ken and Emi. Choose the most appropriate answer to each question.**

1. What does Ken want to do?
   a. Stay home tomorrow.
   b. Go home as soon as possible.
   c. Eat something.
   d. Take some medicine.

2. What does Ken not want to do?
   a. Go home now.
   b. Stay home tomorrow.
   c. Take medicine.
   d. Eat something.

C **You will listen once to a conversation between Ken and Emi. Choose the most appropriate answer to each question.**

1. What happened to Ken?
   a. He has a headache.
   b. He has a stomachache.
   c. He is very tired.
   d. He is very sleepy.

2. What does Ken not want to do?
   a. eat
   b. study
   c. take medicine
   d. practice

D **You will listen once to a conversation between Ken and Emi. Choose the most appropriate answer to each question.**

1. What happened to Emi?
   a. She has a headache.
   b. She has a toothache.
   c. She is very tired.
   d. She is disappointed.

2. What kind of sport did Emi do this morning?
   a. tennis
   b. swimming
   c. basketball
   d. track

E You will listen once to a conversation between Ken and Emi. Choose the most appropriate answer to each question.

1. Where was Ken's game?
   a. at a college
   b. at a high school
   c. at a middle school
   d. at a park

2. When was Emi's game?
   a. yesterday
   b. the day before yesterday
   c. last Saturday
   d. last week

3. Whose team won?
   a. Ken's
   b. Emi's
   c. Both Ken's and Emi's
   d. Neither team

4. Who has a game this Saturday?
   a. Ken
   b. Emi
   c. both Ken and Emi
   d. neither Ken nor Emi

F You will listen once to a narrative. Choose the most appropriate answer to each question.

1. When was the game?
   a. last weekend
   b. the day before yesterday
   c. last month
   d. last night

2. When did the game start?
   a. 7:00 pm
   b. 7:30 pm
   c. 8:00 pm
   d. 8:30 pm

3. Which statement about the game is true?
   a. The other team won, but it was a good game.
   b. His team won and it was a good game.
   c. His team did not do well at all.
   d. The other team was too weak.

4. How did the speaker feel after the game?
   a. He was happy.
   b. He was disappointed.
   c. He was too tired.
   d. He was sick.

G You will listen once to a narrative. Choose the most appropriate answer to each question.

1. When did Emi get sick?
   a. Friday
   b. Saturday
   c. Sunday
   d. Monday

2. What symptoms did Emi have?
   a. a high fever and a sore throat
   b. a sore throat and a stomach ache
   c. a sore throat and a headache
   d. a headache and a stomach ache

3. What did she NOT do during her illness?
   a. She ate a little.
   b. She drank a lot of water.
   c. She went to see a doctor.
   d. She slept.

4. Why does she NOT want to miss school?
   a. There is a swim meet.
   b. There is a math exam.
   c. There is a science exam.
   d. There is a concert.

Ⓐ **Practice Verb TE forms**

In the first blank, indicate if the verb is in Group 1, 2, or 3 by writing the appropriate number. Then write the English meaning in the ( ) and the correct TE form in the last column.

Group		Meaning		TE form
Ex. __1__	かえります	(to return	) →	__かえって__
1. _____	のみます	(	) →	_____
2. _____	行きます	(	) →	_____
3. _____	はじめます	(	) →	_____
4. _____	います	(	) →	_____
5. _____	食べます	(	) →	_____
6. _____	かきます	(	) →	_____
7. _____	よみます	(	) →	_____
8. _____	します	(	) →	_____
9. _____	はなします	(	) →	_____
10. _____	見ます	(	) →	_____
11. _____	来ます	(	) →	_____
12. _____	あるきます	(	) →	_____
13. _____	おきます	(	) →	_____
14. _____	ねます	(	) →	_____
15. _____	言います	(	) →	_____

B Match the Japanese sentence with its correct translation by writing the correct number in the ( ). Then, match the sentence with its correct grammatical function by writing the correct number in the [ ].

		TRANSLATION	FUNCTION
1. のんで　ください。	( )A. May I drink?	[ ]A. Sequence
2. のんでも　いいですか。	( )B. I drank and ate.	[ ]B. Request
3. のんで、食べました。	( )C. Please drink.	[ ]C. Asking permission

C Write the correct TE form of the verb given in the ( ).
Then translate the sentence into English.

Ex. 毎日　（およいで）ください。(およぎます)　　Please swim every day.

1. 八時に　（　　　　）も　いいですか。(来ます) ＿＿＿＿＿＿＿＿＿＿

2. かんじを　（　　　　）、よみました。(かきます) ＿＿＿＿＿＿＿＿＿＿

3. ゆっくり　（　　　　）ください。(はしります) ＿＿＿＿＿＿＿＿＿＿

4. テレビを　（　　　　）、ねました。(見ます) ＿＿＿＿＿＿＿＿＿＿

5. おそく　（　　　　）も　いいですか。(おきます) ＿＿＿＿＿＿＿＿＿＿

D カタカナをかきましょう。

1. shopping (*shoppingu*)　＿＿＿＿＿＿　　　　6. shirt (*shatsu*)　＿＿＿＿＿＿

2. supermarket (*suupaa*)　＿＿＿＿＿＿　　　7. socks (*sokkusu*)　＿＿＿＿＿＿

3. department store (*depaato*)　＿＿＿＿＿＿　8. shoes (*shuuzu*)　＿＿＿＿＿＿

4. cash (*kyasshu*)　＿＿＿＿＿＿　　　　　　9. jacket (*jaketto*)　＿＿＿＿＿＿

5. convenience store (*konbini*)　＿＿＿＿＿＿　10. shorts (*shootsu*)　＿＿＿＿＿＿

Ⓐ Change each verb to the TE + ください form, then translate the sentence into English.

Ex. 田中さんと　はなします。

[TE form + ください]　　[English]

田中さんと　はなして　ください。 Please talk with Mr. Tanaka.

1. 早く　おきます。

　_____

2. ばんごはんを　食べます。

　_____

3. 毎あさ　ジュースを　のみます。

　_____

4. コンピューターの　おみせへ　行きます。

　_____

5. 日本語の　べんきょうを　します。

　_____

6. 四時に　うちへ　かえります。

　_____

7. 白い　犬を　見ます。

　_____

B Fill in the blanks with an appropriate verb in its TE form.

1. すみません。　もう　一ど　（　　　　　　　　）　ください。

2. トイレヘ　（　　　　　　　　）も　いいですか。

3. お水を　（　　　　　　　　）も　いいですか。

4. あついですねえ。　まどを　（　　　　　　　　）　ください。

5. そとは　うるさいですねえ。　ドアを　（　　　　　　　　）　ください。

6. 先生：「しゅくだいを　（　　　　　　　　）　ください。」

　　　生徒：「すみません。　しゅくだいを　うちに　わすれました。」

C In each of the situations below, provide an appropriate response using the TE + ください form.

Ex. What would you say to a student who doesn't prepare for exams?　　→
　　べんきょうして　ください。

1. What would you say to encourage a guest to have some dinner?

_____

2. What would you say to someone who has a very important soccer game next week?

_____

3. What would you say to a student who is speaking English in a Japanese language class?

_____

4. What would you say to someone you want to invite to your home tomorrow?

_____

5. What would you say to someone who is talking loudly in the library?

_____

A Choose the correct translation from the choices given and write the letter in the ( ).

( ) 1. シャツと　パンツを　かいます。 　　A. I will buy either a shirt or pants.

( ) 2. シャツか　パンツを　かいます。 　　B. I will buy both a shirt and pants.

( ) 3. シャツも　パンツも　かいます。 　　C. I will buy a shirt and pants.

( ) 4. シャツも　パンツも　かいません。 　　D. I won't buy either a shirt or pants.

B Write the correct particle, or **X** if no particle is needed, in the ( ) based on the English cues. Do not use は.

1. 私は　テニス（ 　 ）　ダンス（ 　 ）　好きです。
   (I like both tennis and dancing.)

2. きっさてんで　コーヒー（ 　 ）　ジュース（ 　 ）　のみませんか。
   (Won't you drink coffee or juice at the coffee shop?)

3. コンビニ（ 　 ）　はなや（ 　 ）　行きました。
   (I went to the convenience store and the flower shop).

4. スーパーで　パン（ 　 ）　ジャム（ 　 ）　かいました。
   (I bought both bread and jam at the supermarket.)

5. ハンバーガー（ 　 ）　ピザ（ 　 ）　好きでは　ありません。
   (I don't like either hamburgers or pizza.)

6. 私は　白い（ 　 ）　くつ（ 　 ）　かいたいです。
   (I want to buy white shoes.)

7. 私は　きれい（ 　 ）　ドレス（ 　 ）　好きです。
   (I like the pretty dress.)

8. 私は　あか（ 　 ）　白（ 　 ）　シャツを　かいました。
   (I bought the red and white shirt.)

C Choose an appropriate verb and write the correct TE form in each ( ).

1. 生徒: 先生、 すみません、今 トイレに ( ) も いいですか。

   先生: いいです。 でも、きょうしつに 早く ( ) ください。

2. 先生: 今、日本語の 本を ( ) ください。

   生徒: 先生、そとが うるさいです。 ドアを ( ) も

   いいですか。

3. 生徒: 先生、今 おひるごはんを ( ) も いいですか。

   先生: だめです。 でも、お水は ( ) も いいですよ。

D Write the correct Japanese words in the ( ) using the English cues. In the [ ], write the location where you suggest getting the item.

Ex. (白い 犬)を かいたいです。   (white dog)

   そうですか。 じゃ、[ペットショップ]へ 行きましょう。

1. ( )が ほしいです。   (good watch)

   そうですか。 じゃ、[ ]へ 行きましょう。

2. ( )が 食たべたいです。   (delicious sushi)

   そうですか。 じゃ、[ ]へ 行きましょう。

3. ( )を かいたいです。   (pretty flowers)

   そうですか。 じゃ、[ ]へ 行きましょう。

4. ( )を かいたいです。   (a book I like)

   そうですか。 じゃ、[ ]へ 行きましょう。

A Read the following sentences and determine how much the person needs to pay.

1. 毎日　えき (train station) で　英語の　しんぶんと　スポーツしんぶんを
かいます。　英語の　しんぶんは　200円で、スポーツしんぶんは
90円です。　ぜんぶで　いくらですか。　＿＿＿＿＿＿＿＿です。

2. 明日　ともだちと　えいがに　行きます。　きっぷは
一まい　6ドル50セントです。　二まいで　いくらですか。
＿＿＿＿＿＿＿＿です。

3. きのう　あきはばら*へ　行きました。　スマートフォンは　65,000円
でした。　好きな　ケースは　9,000円でした。　イヤフォンは
3,000円でした。　いくらですか。　＿＿＿＿＿＿＿＿です。

* あきはばら is the name of the area in Tokyo where hundreds of discount shops sell cameras, electric appliances, TVs, computers, computer games, and other electronic goods.

B The following is a conversation between a store clerk and a customer.
Complete each sentence according to the English cues.

Clerk:　　　いらっしゃいませ。

Customer:　あの　あかい　シャツは ＿＿＿＿＿＿＿＿＿＿＿＿ (How much?)。

Clerk:　　　＿＿＿＿＿＿＿＿＿＿＿＿＿＿＿＿＿＿ (Which one is it?)。

Customer:　あれですよ。

Clerk:　　　あれは ＿＿＿＿＿＿＿＿＿＿＿＿＿＿＿＿ ($14.50)。

Customer:　高いですね。　じゃ、あの ＿＿＿＿＿＿＿＿＿＿ (yellow one) を

　　　　　　＿＿＿＿＿＿＿＿＿＿＿＿＿＿＿＿＿＿ (Please show me)。

C **Calculate how much money you should give to the clerk and how much change you should receive in the following situations.**

Use the coins and bills shown in the wallet below. Draw the coins and bills you will hand to the clerk for each purchase and the change you will receive. Try to use as few coins/bills as possible.

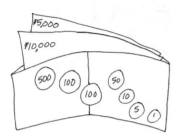

	Money given to clerk	Change received
Ex.	(100) (50)	(10) (10)

Ex. 私： ガムを ください。

いくらですか。

みせの人：ガムは　130円です。

1. 私： ノートを　一さつ　ください。

いくらですか。

みせの人： 180円です。

2. 私： えんぴつを　一本ください。

いくらですか。

みせの人： 25円です。

3. 私： しゃしんは　いくらですか。

みせの人： 720円です。

4. 私： この　くつを　ください。　いくらですか。

みせの人： 3,800円です。

A Choose the most appropriate conjunction from the choices given in the ( ) to form a meaningful sentence.

1. つかれました（A. から　B. 。でも　C. 。それに）、　ちょっと　休みましょう。

2. 先生は　やさしいです（A. 。それに　B. から　C. が）、　いい先生です。

3. 今朝　6時30分に　学校へ　来ました（A. が　B. 。でも

　　C. 。それから）、　ロッカーへ　行きました。

4. テニスが　とくいです（A. が　B. 。そして　C. から）、　水えいは

　　にが手です。

5. はなは　はなやで　かいましょうか。（A. そして　B. それから

　　C. それとも）、　スーパーで　かいましょうか。

B Read the following dialogue between a customer and a clerk in an art gallery. Fill in the blanks based on the English cues given.

アートギャラリーで

Clerk: この　きいろい　はなの　えは _____(how?) ですか。

Customer: _____(wonderful) ですね。　_____(how much?) ですか。

Clerk: _____($2,500) です。

Customer: _____ (Wow! It is very expensive!)

_____ (Please show me the red one.)

Clerk: 分かりました。

C テキストチャット

You will participate in a simulated exchange of text messages. You should respond as fully and as appropriately as possible.

You will have a conversation with Ms. Kawamoto, a high school student in Japan, who wants to know about school lunches in your country.

1. 川本: はじめまして。　川本です。　どうぞ　よろしく。

   Start the conversation.

   _____

2. 川本: たいてい　おひるごはんに　何を　食べますか。
   何を　のみますか。

   Respond.

   _____

3. 川本: 学校の　おひるごはんは　いくらぐらいですか。

   Respond.

   _____

4. 川本: 学校の　カフェテリアの　食べものは　どうですか。

   Provide two comments.

   _____

5. 川本: そうですか。　おひるごはんを　きょうしつで　食べても
   いいですか。

   Respond.

   _____

6. 川本: どうも　ありがとうございました。　また　チャットを　しても
   いいですか。

   End the conversation.

   _____

You may not know all the Japanese you hear, but use what you do know along with your imagination!

A **You will listen once to a narrative. Choose the most appropriate answer to each question.**

1. What is the speaker describing in this passage?
   a. what he did yesterday
   b. his family
   c. his school
   d. his friends

2. What did he NOT purchase?
   a. coffee
   b. watch
   c. book
   d. chocolate

3. What did he purchase at the florist?
   a. one red flower
   b. three purple flowers
   c. three red flowers
   d. one purple flower

4. Which location was crowded?
   a. bookstore
   b. coffee shop
   c. supermarket
   d. sushi shop

B **You will listen once to a conversation between a customer and a store clerk. Choose the most appropriate answer to each question.**

1. What does the customer want to purchase?
   a. a pair of shoes
   b. a watch
   c. flowers
   d. a telephone

2. What color was the product he bought?
   a. red
   b. blue and red
   c. red and white
   d. blue and white

3. How much did it cost?
   a. $45
   b. $54
   c. $39.80
   d. $38.90

4. Why did he buy it?
   a. because of its color
   b. because of its price
   c. because of its appearance
   d. because of its size

C **You will listen once to a conversation between Ken and Emi. Choose the most appropriate answer to each question.**

1. Where are Ken and Emi?
   a. at a department store
   b. at a supermarket
   c. at a shoe shop
   d. at a coffee shop

2. How do they describe the place?
   a. crowded
   b. new and pretty
   c. expensive
   d. interesting

flip over ⇨

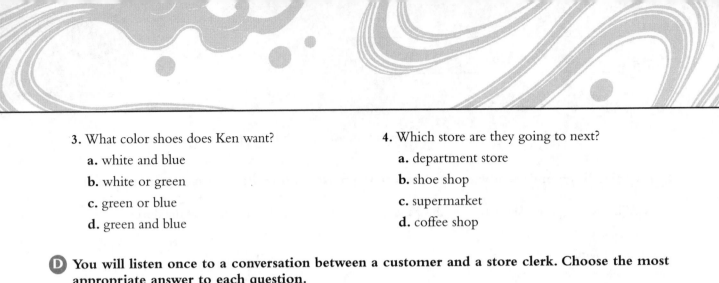

3. What color shoes does Ken want?

    a. white and blue

    b. white or green

    c. green or blue

    d. green and blue

4. Which store are they going to next?

    a. department store

    b. shoe shop

    c. supermarket

    d. coffee shop

D You will listen once to a conversation between a customer and a store clerk. Choose the most appropriate answer to each question.

1. How much is a piece of chocolate?

    a. $1.50

    b. $3.50

    c. $4.00

    d. $7.00

2. How many pieces of chocolate did the customer buy?

    a. one

    b. two

    c. three

    d. four

3. How many orange juices did he order?

    a. one

    b. two

    c. three

    d. four

4. How much was the orange juice?

    a. $5.00

    b. $4.00

    c. $3.50

    d. $7.00

E You will listen once to a conversation between a teacher and her students. Choose the most appropriate answer to each question.

1. What did the teacher ask one of her students to do after everyone sat down?

    a. to turn the lights on

    b. to close the door

    c. to turn in the homework

    d. to close the windows

2. Which statement is true?

    a. Emi forgot her homework and will turn it in tomorrow.

    b. Ken forgot his homework and will turn it in tomorrow.

    c. Ken forgot his homework and will turn it in next week.

    d. Emi forgot her homework and will turn it in next week.

3. What did the teacher have to say to the students twice?

    a. to be quiet

    b. to repeat themselves

    c. to show her their homework

    d. to sit down

4. What did Emi do for the teacher?

    a. She opened the window.

    b. She closed the door.

    c. She closed the window.

    d. She closed both the door and the window.

名前 _____

日づけ _____ _____ 曜日

A Reading a Letter

This is a letter from Ken's Japanese friend. Based on this letter, answer the questions below by circling the correct response for 1 to 3, and answering the questions to 4 and 5 in complete sentences.

こんにちは。おげんきですか。
日本は 今 はるですが、まだ
すこし さむいです。きのう
さくらの はなが とても
きれいでした。
　今 はる休みです。学校は
四月十日から はじまります。
私は 今年から 高校一年生です。
明日 あたらしい きょうかしょを
かいます。アメリカの はる休
みは、いつから いつまでですか。
ケンさんは はる休みに 何を
しましたか。
　きのう ともだちと いっし
よに スーパーマンの えいがを
見ました。おもしろかったです。
ケンさんは 何の えいがが
好きですか。
　また、手がみを かいて
ください。おげんきで。
さようなら。
　　　　　四月五日
　　　　　　山田はな子
ケン・スミスさま*

* さま= さん　[さま is a formal equivalent of さん used in letter writing.]

1. 日本は　もう　はるですか。

　（A. はい　B. いいえ）、（A. もう　はるです　B. まだです）。

2. 日本は　もう　あついですか。

　（A. はい　B. いいえ）、（A. もう　あついです　B. まだです）。

3. はな子さんの　はる休みは　もう　おわりましたか。

　（A. はい　B. いいえ）、（A. もう　おわりました　B. まだです）。

4. はな子さんは　もう　きょうかしょを　かいましたか。

_____

5. はな子さんは　もう　高校生ですか。

_____

B Writing a Response Letter

Ken wrote a reply to Hanako's letter from the previous page. Fill in the ( ) with the correct response chosen from the choices below. Write your own correct answers in the blanks.

はな子さん、　手がみを　ありがとうございました。　ぼくは　（　）です。
ここも　まだ　すこし　（　）ですが、　はなが　（　）ですよ。
　　ぼくの　はる休みは　＿＿月＿＿＿日から　＿＿月＿＿＿日まで
でした。　かぞくと　ボストンに　（　）しました。　とても　（　）です。
　　ぼくの　好きな　えいがは　＿＿＿＿＿＿＿＿です。
　　また、　手がみを　ください。　おげんきで。　さようなら。

ケン

（ a. りょこう　 b. さむい　 c. きれい　　 d. げんき　 e. たのしかった ）

C Propose an appropriate activity in the blanks based on Ken's comments.

1. ケン: おなかが　すきました。

   エミ: そうですか。　じゃ、＿＿＿＿＿＿＿＿＿＿を　食べましょう。

2. ケン: のどが　かわきました。

   エミ: そうですか。　じゃ、＿＿＿＿＿＿＿＿＿＿＿＿＿＿。

3. ケン: 今日　大じな　サッカーの　しあいが　あります。

   エミ: そうですか。　じゃ、＿＿＿＿＿＿＿＿＿＿＿＿＿＿。

4. ケン: よく　はしりましたから、　とても　つかれて　います。

   エミ: そうですか。　じゃ、＿＿＿＿＿＿＿＿＿＿＿＿＿＿。

A **Combine each pair of sentences into one sentence. Translate the new sentence into English.**

Ex. ピザは　3ドルです。　そして、　コーラは　75セントです。

<u>ピザは　3ドルで、　コーラは　85セントです。</u>

<u>Pizza is three dollars and cola is 85 cents.</u>

1. 父は　コックです。　そして、　母は　先生です。

_____

_____

2. あねは　高校三年生です。　そして、　サッカーが　とても
上手です。

_____

_____

3. この　えは　ゆうめいです。　そして、　とても　たかいです。

_____

_____

B **Fill in the blanks with the correct answer using the appropriate counters and the totalizing particle で. Write your answers in *hiragana*.**

Ex. べんとうは　一つ　五ドルでした。

 _____ ふたつで _____ 十ドルでした。

1. シャツは　一まい　十六ドルでした。

　　_____　三十ニドルでした。

2. さかなは　一ぴき　七ドルでした。

　　_____　ニ十一ドルでした。

3. バラ(rose)の　はなは　一本　一ドルニ十五セントでした。

　　_____　七ドル五十セントでした。

4. おにぎりは　一つ　ハ十セントでした。

　　_____　六ドル四十セントでした。

5. ふるい　コンピューターは　一だい　千ドルでした。

　　_____　三千ドルでした。

6. ハンバーガーは　一ドル五十セントでした。　ジュースは

　　一ドルでした。　サラダは　ニドル十セントでした。

　　_____　四ドル六十セントでした。

C Fill in the blanks with the appropriate adjective form and the item it describes.

expensive	cheap	new	old	quiet	noisy
$500	$10	$800	$400	$160	$190

1. _やすい　とけい_は　十ドルで、_____は　五百ドルです。

2. _____は　ハ百ドルで、_____は　四百ドルです。

3. _____は　百六十ドルで、_____は　百九十ドルです。

A Fill in the blanks with the means by which you do each of the following things.

Ex. 私は　この　しゅくだいを　___えんぴつ___　で　かきます。

1. 私は　おべんとうを　_____で　食べます。

2. 私は　ハンバーガーを　_____で　食べます。

3. 私は　サラダを　_____で　食べます。

4. 私は　ステーキ (steak) を　_____と　_____で

食べます。

5. 私は　英語の　レポートを　_____で　タイプします。

6. 私は　学校へ　_____で　来ます。

7. ゆうべ　私は　ともだちと　_____で　はなしました。

B Fill in the blanks with the correct counters in *hiragana*, using the cues given in the ( ).

Ex. のどが　かわきました。　お水を　___いっぱい___　ください。(1)

1. すみません、　おべんとうを　_____　ください。(2)

2. すみません、　コーヒーを　_____　ください。(3)

3. コンピューターを　_____　かいました。(1)

4. すみません、　かみを　_____　ください。(1)

5. うちに　小さい　とりが　_____　います。(2)

6. すみません、　ストローを　_____　ください。(1)

C Fill in the blanks with the appropriate Japanese phrases, based on the English cues.

ケン: ああ、おなかが ＿＿＿＿＿＿＿＿＿＿＿＿＿＿ (empty, "hungry") 。

まりさんは ＿＿＿＿＿＿＿＿＿ (already) おひるごはんを

食べましたか。

まり: いいえ、＿＿＿＿＿＿＿＿＿ (not yet) です。

ケン: じゃ、いっしょに おひるごはんを ＿＿＿＿＿＿＿＿＿ (Won't you eat?)

まり: はい、＿＿＿＿＿＿＿＿＿＿＿＿＿ (let's eat) 。

<ファーストフードの おみせで>

ケン: すみません、＿＿＿＿＿＿＿＿＿＿＿＿＿＿＿ (hamburger) と

＿＿＿＿＿＿＿＿＿＿＿＿＿＿＿ (soda = sooda) を ください。

おみせの 人: ソーダの サイズは 何ですか。

ケン: ＿＿＿＿＿＿＿＿＿＿＿＿ (a large one) を ください。

ぼくは のどが ＿＿＿＿＿＿＿＿＿＿＿ (dry, "thirsty") 。

まり: 私は ＿＿＿＿＿＿＿ (rice ball) と ＿＿＿＿＿＿＿ (salad) と

＿＿＿＿＿＿＿＿＿ (ice tea = aisutii) を ください。

おみせの 人: ＿＿＿＿＿＿＿ (for all) ＿＿＿＿＿ ($12.50) です。

ありがとう ございました。

<テーブルで>

ケン: あっ、＿＿＿＿＿＿＿ (straw) を ＿＿＿＿＿＿＿＿ (forgot) 。

まりさんも ＿＿＿＿＿＿＿＿＿＿＿＿ (do you need?) 。

まり: いいえ、＿＿＿＿＿＿＿＿＿＿＿ (no, thank you) 。

A Combine each pair of sentences into one sentence. Then, translate the entire sentence into English.

Ex. ピザは　つめたいです。　そして、　まずいです。

ピザは　つめた(くて、)　まずいです。

The pizza is cold and does not taste good.

1. しけんは　ながいです。　そして、　むずかしいです。

_____

_____

2. 日本語は　おもしろいです。　そして、　たのしいです。

_____

_____

3. *母の*　おべんとうは　あたたかかったです。　そして、

おいしかったです。

_____

_____

4. レストランの　食べものは　たかかったです。　そして、

まずかったです。

_____

_____

5. 科学の　先生は　きれいです。　そして、　やさしいです。

_____

_____

B Matching: What should you say in Japanese? Write the letter from the right column in the appropriate ( ).

1. before a meal?   (   )

2. after a meal?   (   )

3. when you are full?   (   )

4. when you are hungry?   (   )

5. when you are thirsty?   (   )

6. when you want to know the total cost?   (   )

7. when you order one hamburger?   (   )

8. when you offer someone another cup of coffee?   (   )

9. when you want to decline an offer?   (   )

A. おなかが　いっぱいです。

B. ぜんぶで　いくらですか。

C. のどが　カラカラです。

D. いいえ、　けっこうです。

E. いただきます。

F. おなかが　ペコペコです。

G. もう　いっぱい　どうぞ。

H. ひとつ　ください。

I. ごちそうさま。

よみましょう!　**Let's read!**

Circle the correct answers based on the reading.

1. Which statement is true?

   a. Her mother makes her lunch every day.

   b. Her school lunch is expensive.

   c. Her school lunch is cold.

   d. Her mother's lunch is cold.

2. What is the writer not pleased about?

   a. The writer had to use her hands to eat lunch.

   b. The writer ate two big rice balls.

   c. The writer ate leftover tempura.

   d. The writer's mother does not make her lunch.

私は　母の　べんとうが　大好きですが、母は　よく　おそく　おきますから、私は　たいてい　学校で　ランチを　かいます。学校の　ランチは　あたたかくて、やすいですが、あまり　おいしくないです。母の　おべんとうは　つめたいですが、おいしいです。今日の　母の　おべんとうは　おにぎり　二つと　天ぷらでした。おはしを　わすれましたから、私は　おべんとうを　手で　食べました。良くないですね。

名前 _____

日づけ _____ _____ 曜日

A The pictures tell you what Ken did yesterday. In one sentence, state both activities he did.

6:00 a.m.　　　6:15 a.m.

Ex.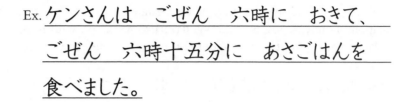
ケンさんは　ごぜん　六時に　おきて、
ごぜん　六時十五分に　あさごはんを
食べました。

8:00 a.m.　　　8:30 a.m.

1. ケンさんは _____

_____

4:00 p.m.　　　before 7 p.m.

2. ケンさんは _____

_____

7:30 p.m.　　　around 8:30 p.m.

3. ケンさんは _____

_____

10:00 p.m.　　　after 11 p.m.

4. ケンさんは _____

_____

B How do you say the following in Japanese?

1. See you later. (to your friend) _____

2. Good-bye. (to your friend) _____

You will participate in a simulated exchange of text-chat messages. You should respond as fully and as appropriately as possible. You will have a conversation with Kenji Mizuguchi, a high school student in Japan who wants to know about fast food restaurants in your country.

1. 水口: はじめまして。　水口です。　高校一年で、　16さいです。
   どうぞ　よろしく。

   Start the conversation.

   _____

2. 水口: どの　ファストフードの　おみせに　行きますか。

   Respond and state one reason.

   _____

2. 水口: そうですか。　そこで　たいてい　何を　食べて、　何を
   のみますか。

   Respond.

   _____

3. 水口: そうですか。　その　食べものと　のみものは、
   いくらぐらいですか。

   Respond.

   _____

5. 水口: 分かりました。　ファストフードが　好きですか。

   Respond and state two reasons.

   _____

6. 水口: どうも　ありがとう　ございました。　たのしかったです。
   これから　ときどき　チャットを　しましょう。　おげんきで。

   End the conversation.

   _____

Write a composition about an event that occurred this past year. Tell who you did the activity with, when it happened, and where it was. Describe the event and add your opinion of the activity. Explain what you did using at least three conjoining sentences. Be sure to use correct past tense forms. Use transitional words, such as それから、でも、そして、etc. Use *kanji* wherever possible. Begin and end your composition appropriately and include an appropriate title.

Possible topics: School events, sporting events, travel, illness, special weekend/family events, holidays, etc.

Write neatly and legibly.

_____

_____

_____

_____

_____

_____

_____

_____

_____

_____

You may not know all the Japanese you hear, but use what you do know along with your imagination!

A You will listen once to a conversation between Ken and Emi. Choose the most appropriate answer to each question.

1. Why is Ken busy now?
   a. because of a social studies exam
   b. because of an English paper
   c. because of his reading for classes
   d. because of his social studies paper

2. What has he done already?
   a. He has already studied for an exam.
   b. He has already written a paper for a class.
   c. He has already read a book.
   d. He has already eaten lunch.

3. What are they going to do together?
   a. study
   b. do homework
   c. eat lunch
   d. drink coffee

4. Where are they going to go?
   a. cafeteria
   b. coffee shop
   c. restaurant
   d. classroom

B You will listen once to a conversation between a customer and a store clerk. Choose the most appropriate answer to each question.

1. Which food did the customer order?
   a. one hamburger and small fries
   b. two hamburgers and small fries
   c. one hamburger and medium fries
   d. two hamburgers and medium fries

2. What drinks did he order?
   a. two small colas
   b. one small cola and one medium cola
   c. one medium cola and one large cola
   d. one small cola and one large cola

3. How much was one hamburger?
   a. $1.00
   b. $1.75
   c. $2.00
   d. $2.50

4. What was the total cost of the order?
   a. $9.25
   b. $9.75
   c. $10.00
   d. $10.25

C You will listen once to a conversation between Ken and Emi. Choose the most appropriate answer to each question.

1. How were Ken and Emi's hamburgers?
   a. large and delicious
   b. cold and unappetizing
   c. warm and delicious
   d. small and unappetizing

2. How were the fries?
   a. cold and delicious
   b. cold and unappetizing
   c. warm and delicious
   d. small and unappetizing

flip over ⇨

3. How were their drinks?

    a. cold and delicious

    b. hot and delicious

    c. cold and not good

    d. warm and not good

4. What did Emi eat?

    a. a hamburger only

    b. a hamburger and one fry

    c. fries only

    d. nothing, she only had a drink

D You will listen once to Emi talking to her friends. Choose the most appropriate answer to each question.

1. When is Ken's birthday?

    a. yesterday

    b. today

    c. tomorrow

    d. the day after tomorrow

2. What day is his birthday?

    a. April 8th

    b. April 20th

    c. July 8th

    d. July 20th

3. Where is the party?

    a. at Ken's house

    b. at Emi's house

    c. at Emi's friend's house

    d. at school

4. How are they going to eat their food?

    a. with chopsticks

    b. with forks and by hand

    c. with chopsticks and by hand

    d. by hand only

E You will listen once to a conversation between Ken and Emi. Choose the most appropriate answer to each question.

1. What does Ken have next?

    a. English class

    b. break

    c. math class

    d. science class

2. What is Emi going to do at the library?

    a. read and write a paper

    b. read and study for a test

    c. write a paper and study for a test

    d. meet her friends and study for a test

3. What are Ken and Emi doing after school together?

    a. participating in sports and going to a coffee shop

    b. going to a coffee shop and studying

    c. going to a coffee shop and going home

    d. studying at a library and going to a coffee shop

4. What are they going to have at the coffee shop?

    a. Both Ken and Emi will drink hot coffee.

    b. Both Ken and Emi will drink iced coffee.

    c. Ken will drink hot coffee and Emi will drink iced coffee.

    d. Emi will drink hot coffee and Ken will drink iced coffee.

ひらがな

Start from the right column. s = stop, t = tail, h = hook.

↓

O	E	U ★	I	A
お	え	う	い	あ

*う is used in writing the second O in the long vowel sound OO. Ex. どうぞ *doozo*,
さようなら *sayoonara*. There are some exceptions you must learn as they are introduced.

よみましょう! **Let's read!**

1.	い	stomach		6.	あお	blue (color)
2.	え	painting		7.	おい	nephew
3.	お	tail		8.	うえ	up, above
4.	あい	love		9.	ええ	yes
5.	いえ	house		10.	いいえ	no

かきましょう! **Let's write!**

A Write A, I, U, E, O horizontally and vertically five times each without looking at the chart.

a. horizontally

A	I	U	E	O

b. vertically

					A
					I
					U
					E
					O

B Write the words in *hiragana*.

1. Yes (Informal)   _____   _____
                           e   e

2. No   _____   _____   _____
              i   i   e

Start from the right column. s = stop, t = tail, h = hook.

↓

KO	KE	KU	KI	KA
こ	け	く	き	か
こ	け	く	き	か
こ	け	く	き	か

Start from the right column. s = stop, t = tail, h = hook   ↓

GO	GE	GU	GI	GA
ご	げ	ぐ	ぎ	が
	げ	ぐ	ぎ	が
	げ	ぐ	ぎ	が

なまえ *Namae* (Name) _____

ひづけ *Hizuke* (Date) _____ _____ ようび *Yoobi*
(Day of the week)

 よみましょう! **Let's read!**

1.	あき	autumn, fall		6.	かお	face	
2.	かい	seashell		7.	かぎ	key	
3.	いけ	pond		8.	かげ	shadow	
4.	こい	carp		9.	けいこ	Keiko (Japanese girl's name)	
5.	きかい	machine		10.	あきお	Akio (Japanese boy's name)	

 かきましょう! **Let's write!**

A Write A, I, U, E, O, KA, KI, KU, KE, KO, GA, GI, GU, GE, GO vertically THREE times each without looking at the chart.

G	K		
			A
			I
			U
			E
			O

G	K		
			A
			I
			U
			E
			O

G	K		
			A
			I
			U
			E
			O

B Write these names in *hiragana*.

1. Aoki (Family) _____ _____ _____

2. Ueki (Family) _____ _____ _____

3. Akagi (Family) _____ _____ _____

4. Keiko (Female) _____ _____ _____

5. Kikuko (Female) _____ _____ _____

6. Akio (Male) _____ _____ _____

ORIGINS OF
Hiragana

Part 1

All of the symbols of the *hiragana* are derived originally from Chinese characters. Here are the original Chinese characters from which each *hiragana* developed and their three different styles of penmanship. In each group, the first column on the left shows the modern *kana* symbol; the second column shows the *kanji* from which that *kana* was derived, with the *kanji* written in KAISHO style (regular style); the third column shows the same *kanji* in GYOOSHO style (walking style); and the fourth column shows the *kanji* in SOOSHO style (grass style).

	Hiragana	Kaisho	Gyoosho	Soosho		Hiragana	Kaisho	Gyoosho	Soosho
A	あ	安	安	あ	KA	か	加	加	か
I	い	以	以	い	KI	き	幾	幾	き
U	う	宇	宇	う	KU	く	久	久	く
E	え	衣	衣	え	KE	け	計	計	け
O	お	於	於	お	KO	こ	己	己	こ

Start from the right column. s = stop, t = tail, h = hook.   ↓

SO	SE	SU	SHI	SA
そ	せ	す	し	さ
そ そ	せ せ	す す	し し	さ さ

なまえ *Namae* (Name) _____

ひづけ *Hizuke* (Date) _____ _____ ようび *Yoobi*
(Day of the week)

Start from the right column. s = stop, t = tail, h = hook. ↓

ZO		ZE		ZU		JI		ZA	
	ぞ		ぜ		ず		じ		ざ
	ぞ		ぜ		ず		じ		ざ

よみましょう! **Let's read!**

1.	おすし	sushi (polite)	6.	うし	cow
2.	おかし	sweets; candy	7.	かぜ	a cold
3.	せかい	world	8.	おじ	uncle
4.	ござ	beach mat	9.	すき	like
5.	ぞう	elephant	10.	おさけ	rice wine (polite)

かきましょう! **Let's write!**

A Write A, I, U, E, O, KA, KI, KU, KE, KO, GA, GI, GU, GE, GO, SA, SHI, SU, SE, SO, ZA, JI, ZU, ZE, ZO vertically TWO times each without looking at the chart.

Z	S	G	K		
					A
					I
					U
					E
					O

Z	S	G	K		
					A
					I
					U
					E
					O

B Write the words in *hiragana*.

1. Seki (family name) _____ _____

2. Suzuki (family name) _____ _____ _____

3. Seiko (female name) _____ _____ _____

4. Aosaki (family name) _____ _____ _____ _____

5. Asakusa (town name) _____ _____ _____ _____

6. sushi _____ _____

7. sake (rice wine) _____ _____

8. Saeko (female name) _____ _____ _____

9. four [*shi*] _____

10. five [*go*] _____

Hiragana

Part 2

In each group, the first column on the left shows the modern *kana* symbol; the second column shows the *kanji* from which that *kana* was derived, with the *kanji* written in KAISHO style (regular style); the third column shows the same *kanji* in GYOOSHO style (walking style); and the fourth column shows the *kanji* in SOOSHO style (grass style).

	Hiragana	Kaisho	Gyoosho	Soosho		Hiragana	Kaisho	Gyoosho	Soosho
SA	さ	左	さ	さ	TA	た	太	た	た
SHI	し	え	え	し	CHI	ち	知	知	ち
SU	す	寸	す	す	TSU	つ	川	り	つ
SE	せ	世	せ	せ	TE	て	天	天	て
SO	そ	曽	秀	そ	TO	と	止	止	と

Start from the right column. s = stop, t = tail, h = hook.

↓

TO	TE	TSU	CHI	TA
と	て	っ	ち	た
と	て	っ	ち	た
と	て	っ	ち	た

ひらがな HIRAGANA

Start from the right column. s = stop, t = tail, h = hook.   ↓

DO	DE	ZU *	JI *	DA
ど	で	づ	ぢ	だ
ど	で	づ	ぢ	だ
ど	で	づ	ぢ	だ

*1 ぢ is used only for words relating to the word "blood" (ち).

*2 づ is used following another つ or for a ZU sound which is derived from a word originally
written with a つ. For example, あいづち *aizuchi*.

H4-C
ひらがな

よみましょう! Let's read!

1.	て	hand		6.	おだ	(Family name)
2.	と	door		7.	つだ	(Family name)
3.	ちず	map		8.	たけした	(Family name)
4.	つき	moon		9.	あきた	(Prefecture name)
5.	てつお	(Male name)		10.	たかだ	(Family name)

かきましょう! Let's write!

A Fill in the blanks with the correct *hiragana*.
Use う for the second O sound in a word with the long OO vowel sound.

1. _____ _____ _____ _____ _____ね_____ 。(It's hot!)
　　A　　tsu　　i　　　de　　su　　ne　　e.

_____ _____ _____ _____ね_____ 。(Yes, it is!)
So　　o　　de　　su　　ne　　e.

2. _____ _____ん_____ _____ _____ _____ 。(How are you?)
　O　　ge　　n　　ki　　de　　su　　ka

は_____ 、_____ん_____ _____ _____ 。(Yes, I am fine.)
Ha　i　　　ge　n　　ki　　de　　su

3. _____ _____も_____り_____ _____ _____ 。
　Do　　o　　mo　　a　ri　　ga　　to　　o

_____ _____ _____ま_____ 。(Thank you very much.)
go　　za　　i　ma　　su

_____ _____ _____ _____ _____ま_____ _____ 。(You're welcome.)
Do　　o　　i　　ta　　shi　ma　shi　　te

4. は_____めま_____ _____ 。(How do you do?)
Ha　ji　me　ma　shi　te

わ_____ _____は_____ _____ _____ _____ _____ 。(I am Aoki.)
Wa　ta　　shi　wa　A　　o　　ki　　de　　su

_____ _____ _____よ ろ_____ _____ 。(Nice to meet you.)
Do　　o　　zo　yo　ro　shi　ku

Part 3

In each group, the first column on the left shows the modern *kana* symbol; the second column shows the *kanji* from which that *kana* was derived, with the *kanji* written in KAISHO style (regular style); the third column shows the same *kanji* in GYOOSHO style (walking style); and the fourth column shows the *kanji* in SOOSHO style (grass style).

	Hiragana	Kaisho	Gyoosho	Soosho		Hiragana	Kaisho	Gyoosho	Soosho
NA	な	奈	奈	な	HA	は	波	波	は
NI	に	仁	仁	に	HI	ひ	比	比	ひ
NU	ぬ	奴	ぬ	ぬ	HU	ふ	不	不	ふ
NE	ね	祢	祢	ね	HE	へ	部	乀	へ
NO	の	乃	乃	の	HO	ほ	保	保	ほ

Start from the right column. s = stop, t = tail, h = hook.

↓

ひらがな　HIRAGANA

NO		NE		NU		NI		NA	
	の		ね		ぬ		に		な
	の		ね		ぬ		に		な
	の		ね		ぬ		に		な

なまえ *Namae* (Name) _____

ひづけ *Hizuke* (Date) _____ _____ ようび *Yoobi*
(Day of the week)

よみましょう! **Let's read!**

1.	あなた	you	6.	うなぎ	eel
2.	ねこ	cat	7.	かに	crab
3.	なか	inside	8.	ねぎ	green onion
4.	いぬ	dog	9.	かたな	sword
5.	のど	throat	10.	のぐち	(Family name)

かきましょう! **Let's write!**

A Fill in the blanks with the correct *hiragana*.
Use う for the second O sound of the long OO vowel sound.

1. _____ れ は _____ ん _____ _____ _____。 (What is that over there?)
　　A　re wa　na　n　de　su　ka.

2. _____ _____ _____ _____ _____ _____ _____ _____ _____ _____。 (Please be quiet.)
　Shi　zu　ka　ni　shi　te　ku　da　sa　i.

3. _____ _____ _____ _____ _____ _____ _____ _____。 (It is cool!)
　Su　zu　shi　i　de　su　ne　e.

4. Dog は 、_____ ほん _____ _____ _____ ん _____
　　　　　wa　ni　ho　n　go　de　na　n　to

_____ _____ ま _____ _____。 (How do you say "dog" in Japanese?)
　i　i　ma　su　ka.

5. _____ ん _____ _____ は。 (Good afternoon.)
　Ko　n　ni　chi wa.

6. _____ _____ _____ _____ _____。 (He is tardy.)
　Chi　ko　ku　de　su.

7. _____ _____ _____ (money)
　O　ka　ne

8. _____ よ _____ _____ ら。 (Good-bye.)
　Sa　yo　o　na　ra.

Start from the right column. s = stop, t = tail, h = hook.   ↓

HO	HE *	FU *	HI	HA *
ほ	へ	ふ	ひ	は
ほ	へ	ふ	ひ	は
ほ	へ	ふ	ひ	は

*1 は is also pronounced WA when it is used as a topic particle.

*2 ふ is written as FU in ROOMAJI, but is pronounced like WHO. It is not pronounced as an English "f."

*3 へ is also pronounced E when it is used as a direction particle.

Start from the right column. s = stop, t = tail, h = hook.   ↓

BO	BE	BU	BI	BA
ぼ	べ	ぶ	び	ば
ぼ	べ	ぶ	び	ば
ぼ	べ	ぶ	び	ば

なまえ *Namae* (Name) _____

ひづけ *Hizuke* (Date) _____ _____ ようび *Yoobi*
(Day of the week)

Start from the right column. s = stop, t = tail, h = hook. ↓

PO	PE	PU	PI	PA
ぽ	ぺ	ぶ	ぴ	ぱ
ぽ	ぺ	ぶ	ぴ	ぱ
ぽ	ぺ	ぶ	ぴ	ぱ

ひらがな HIRAGANA

よみましょう! **Let's read!**

1.	は	tooth, teeth		6.	へび	snake
2.	ひと	person		7.	たび	travel, trip
3.	へい	wall		8.	ぶどう	grape
4.	ほし	star		9.	かば	hippo
5.	おばけ	ghost		10.	ばか	stupid, fool

かきましょう! **Let's write!**

A Fill in the blanks with the correct *hiragana*. Use は for the particle **WA**.
Use う for the second **O** of the long **OO** vowel sound.

1. ____ ____ ____ ____ ____   ____ ____ ____ ____
    Ko   no   o   ka   ne   wa (particle)   a   na   ta   no

____ ____ ____ 。 (Is this money yours?)
de   su   ka.

____ ____ 、____ れ ____   わ ____ ____ ____ ____ ____ 。 (Yes, that is mine.)
Ha   i   so   re   wa (particle)   wa   ta   shi   no   de   su.

2. ____ ____ め ま ____ ____ 。 (How do you do?)
   Ha   ji   me   ma   shi   te.

____ ____ ____ ____ ____ ____ ____ 。 (I am Tanabe.)
Bo   ku   wa (particle)   Ta   na   be   de   su.

____ ____ ____ よ ろ ____ ____ 。 (Nice to meet you.)
Do   o   zo   yo ro   shi   ku.

3. ____ ん ____ ____ (pencil)   4. ____ ____ ん ____ (Japanese language)
   e   n   pi   tsu   ni   ho   n   go

5. ____ ____ ____ (hat, cap)   6. ____ や ____ 。 (Hurry up!)
   bo   o   shi   Ha   ya   ku.

7. ____ ____ よ ____ ____ ____ ____ ま ____ 。 (Good morning.)
   O   ha   yo   o   go   za   i   ma   su.

Start from the right column. s = stop, t = tail, h = hook. ↓

MO	ME	MU	MI	MA
も	め	む	み	ま
	も	め	む	み	ま
	も	め	む	み	ま

よみましょう! **Let's read!**

1.	め	eye	6.	むすび	rice ball
2.	みず	water	7.	もち	*mochi*
3.	むし	worm	8.	さしみ	raw fish
4.	なまえ	name	9.	あめ	rain; candy [different pitch]
5.	もしもし	hello [when on the phone]	10.	うめぼし	pickled plum

かきましょう! **Let's write!**

A **Fill in the blanks with the correct *hiragana*.**
Use う for the second O of the long OO vowel sound.

1. ____ ____ を ____ ____ ____ ____ ____ ____ ____ ____ 。 (Please give me one
   Ka mi o i chi ma i ku da sa i.   sheet of paper.)

   ____ ____ 、____ ____ ____ 。 (Here, please.)
   Ha i   do o zo.

2. ____ ____ を ____ ____ ____ ____ ____ ____ ____ 。 (Please give me one piece of
   A me o hi to tsu ku da sa i.   candy.)

3. ____ ____ を ____ ____ ____ ____ ____ ____ ____ 。 (Please open the window.)
   Ma do o a ke te ku da sa i.

   ____ ____ ____ ____ ____ ____ ____ 。 (Please close it.)
   Shi me te ku da sa i.

4. ____ ____ ____ ____ ん 、____ ____ ____ ____ ん。 (Sorry, I cannot see it.)
   Su mi ma se n, mi e ma se n.

5. ____ ____ ____ ____ 。 (It is no good.)
   Da me de su.

6. ____ ____ ____ ____ ____ ____ ____ 。 (It is cold!)
   Sa mu i de su ne e.

Start from the right column. s = stop, t = tail, h = hook.

↓

YO			YU			YA	
よ			ゆ			や	
	よ			ゆ			や
	よ			ゆ			や

ひらがな　HIRAGANA

なまえ *Namae* (Name) _____

ひづけ *Hizuke* (Date) _____ _____
ようび *Yoobi*
(Day of the week)

H8-B
ひらがな

 よみましょう！ **Let's read!**

1.	や	arrow	6.	ようこ	(Female name)
2.	おゆ	hot water	7.	よしこ	(Female name)
3.	ゆき	snow	8.	やまだ	(Family name)
4.	ゆうき	courage	9.	やまもと	(Family name)
5.	ゆめ	dream	10.	よしだ	(Family name)

 かきましょう！ **Let's write!**

A **Fill in the blanks with the correct *hiragana*.**
Use う for the second O of the long OO vowel sound.

1. ____ ____ ____ ____ ____ ____ ____ ____ ____ 。 (Good morning.)
   O   ha   yo   o   go   za   i   ma   su.

2. ____ ____ ____ ____ ん、____ ____ ____ 。 (Yuko, hurry up.)
   Yu   u   ko   sa   n   ha   ya   ku.

3. ____ ____ ____ ____ ____ ____ 。 (He is absent.)
   O   ya   su   mi   de   su.

4. ____ ____ ____ ____ ____ ____ ____ 。 (You did well.)
   Yo   ku   de   ki   ma   shi   ta.

5. ____ ん ____ ____ ____ ____ ____ 。 (Please read.)
   Yo   n   de   ku   da   sa   i.

6. ____ ____ を ____ ____ ____ ____ ____ ____ ____ 。 (Please give me two pieces
   A   me   o   fu   ta   tsu   ku   da   sa   i.   of candy.)

7. ____ ____ ____ ____ ____ ____ 。 (Can you hear?)
   Ki   ko   e   ma   su   ka.

8. ____ ____ ____ ____ ____ ____ ____ 。 (It is cold!)
   Sa   mu   i   de   su   ne   e.

Start from the right column. s = stop, t = tail, h = hook.   ↓

RO	RE	RU	RI	RA
ろ	れ	る	り	ら
ろ	れ	る	り	ら
ろ	れ	る	り	ら

よみましょう! **Let's read!**

1.	あり	ant	6.	よる	night
2.	いろ	color	7.	あられ	rice cracker
3.	りす	squirrel	8.	れきし	history
4.	しろ	castle	9.	こおり	ice
5.	はる	spring	10.	さむらい	samurai

かきましょう! **Let's write!**

A Fill in the blanks with the correct *hiragana*. Use は for the topic particle **WA** and う for the second **O** of the long **OO** vowel sound.

1. ____ ____ ____ ____ ____ ____ 。 ____ ____ ____
   Ha   ji   me   ma   shi   te   Do   o   zo

   ____ ____ ____ ____ 。 (How do you do? Nice to meet you.)
   yo   ro   shi   ku.

2. ____ ____ ____ ____ ____ ____ ____ ____ ____ ____ 。 (Is this yours?)
   Ko   re   wa (P)   a   na   ta   no   de   su   ka.

3. ____ ____ ____ ____ ____ ____ ____ ____ ____ ____ ____ ____ ____ 。 (That eraser
   So   no   ke   shi   go   mu   wa (P)   bo   ku   no   de   su.   is mine.)

4. ____ ____ ____ ____ ____ ____ ____ ____ ____ 。 (Thank you very much.)
   A   ri   ga   to   o   go   za   i   ma   su.

5. ____ ____ ____ ____ ん。 (I do not know.)
   Shi   ri   ma   se   n.

6. ____ ____ を ____ ____ ____ ____ ____ ____ ____ ____ 。 (Please give me one sheet of
   Ka   mi   o   i   chi   ma   i   ku   da   sa   i.   paper.)

7. ____ ____ ____ ____ ____ ____ ん ____ ____ 、
   Ya   ma   mo   to   se   n   se   i

   ____ ____ ____ ____ ____ 。 (Mr./Ms. Yamamoto, good-bye.)
   sa   yo   o   na   ra.

Start from the right column. s = stop, t = tail, h = hook.

↓

	N			O (Particle)			WA
	ん			を			わ
	ん			を			わ
	ん			を			わ

ひらがな HIRAGANA

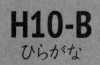

なまえ *Namae* (Name) _____

ひづけ *Hizuke* (Date) _____ _____ ようび *Yoobi*
(Day of the week)

 よみましょう! **Let's read!**

1.	かわ	river	7.	せんそう	war
2.	わし	eagle	8.	べんとう	box lunch
3.	わに	crocodile; alligator	9.	てんぷら	tempura
4.	にわ	garden, yard	10.	わんわん	bow wow
5.	まんが	comics	11.	なっとう	fermented soy bean
6.	みかん	tangerine	12.	てっぽう	gun

 かきましょう! **Let's write!**

Ⓐ Fill in the blanks with the correct *hiragana*. Use は for the topic particle **WA**.

1. ____ ____ ____ ____ ____ ____ ____ ____ ____ 。 (I am Honda.)
Wa　ta　shi　wa (P)　Ho　n　da　de　su.

2. ____ ____ ____ ____ ____ ____ ____ ____ 。 (What is that?)
So　re　wa (P)　na　n　de　su　ka.

3. ____ ____ ____ ____ ____ ____ ____ ____ ____ ____ ____ ____ ____ 。 (Mr./Ms. Yamada, hello.)
Ya　ma　da　se　n　se　i　ko　n　ni　chi　wa. (P)　hello.)

4. ____ ____ ____ ____ ____ ____ ____ ____ ____ ____ ____ 。 (Slowly, please.)
Yu　k　ku　ri　o　ne　ga　i　shi　ma　su.

5. ____ ____ ____ ____ ____ ____ 。 (I do not understand.)
Wa　ka　ri　ma　se　n.

6. ____ ____ ____ ____ ____ ____ ____ ____ 。 (Please give me an exam.)
Shi　ke　n　o (P)　ku　da　sa　i.

7. ____ ____ ____ ____ ____ ____ ____ ____ 。 (Please sit down.)
Su　wa　t　te　ku　da　sa　i.

8. ____ ____ ____ ____ (pencil)
e　n　pi　tsu

9. ____ ____ (book)
ho　n

The small *hiragana* や, ゆ, and よ are only used after *hiragana* in the -I row: that is, き, ぎ, し, じ, ち, に, ひ, び, ぴ, み, and り. When writing vertically on *genkoyoshi*, these small *hiragana* are positioned as follows.

When writing horizontally on *genkoyoshi*, these small *hiragana* are positioned as follows.

1. きゃ KYA	きゅ	KYU	きょ	KYO
2. ぎゃ GYA	ぎゅ	GYU	ぎょ	GYO
3. しゃ SHA	しゅ	SHU	しょ	SHO
4. じゃ JA	じゅ	JU	じょ	JO
5. ちゃ CHA	ちゅ	CHU	ちょ	CHO
6. にゃ NYA	にゅ	NYU	にょ	NYO
7. ひゃ HYA	ひゅ	HYU	ひょ	HYO
8. びゃ BYA	びゅ	BYU	びょ	BYO
9. ぴゃ PYA	ぴゅ	PYU	ぴょ	PYO
10. みゃ MYA	みゅ	MYU	みょ	MYO
11. りゃ RYA	りゅ	RYU	りょ	RYO

よみましょう! **Let's read!**

1. りょこう	travel	
2. しゃしん	photo	
3. びょういん	hospital	
4. きゅうり	cucumber	
5. ぎゅうにゅう	(cow) milk	

6. りゅう	dragon	
7. にんぎょう	doll	
8. ちょうちょう	butterfly	
9. じゅぎょう	class instruction	
10. じゃんけんぽん	*jan-ken-pon* [rock–paper–scissors]	

かきましょう! **Let's write!**

A **Fill in the blanks with the correct *hiragana*.**

1. _____ _____ _____ _____ _____ _____ _____。 (Let's begin.)
    Ha   ji   me   ma   sho   o.

2. _____ _____ _____ _____ _____ _____ _____ _____ 。 (190)
    Hya   ku   kyu   u   ju   u.

3. _____ _____ _____ _____ 。 (Sit down.)
    Cha   ku   se   ki.

4. _____ _____ _____ _____ _____ (text)
    kyo   o   ka   sho

5. _____ _____ _____ (dictionary)
    ji   sho

6. _____ _____ _____ _____ _____ (homework)
    shu   ku   da   i

7. _____ _____ _____ テスト (quiz)
    sho   o   te su to

8. _____ _____ _____ _____ (photo)
    sha   shi   n

9. _____ _____ _____ _____ _____ (China)
    chu   u   go   ku

10. _____ _____ _____ _____ _____ _____ _____ _____ _____ _____ (7th grade)
    chu   u   ga   ku   i   chi   ne   n   se   i

11. _____ _____ _____ _____ _____ _____ (doctor)
    o   i   sha   sa   n

12. _____ _____ _____ (housewife)
    shu   fu

13. _____ _____ _____ _____ (hospital)
    byo   o   i   n

Part 4

	Hiragana	Kaisho	Gyoosho	Soosho
MA	ま	末	ま	ま
MI	み	美	美	み
MU	む	武	武	む
ME	め	女	女	め
MO	も	毛	毛	も

	Hiragana	Kaisho	Gyoosho	Soosho
YA	や	也	也	や
YU	ゆ	由	由	ゆ
YO	よ	与	与	与

	Hiragana	Kaisho	Gyoosho	Soosho
RA	ら	良	良	ら
RI	り	利	利	り
RU	る	留	る	る
RE	れ	禮	礼	礼
RO	ろ	呂	呂	ろ

	Hiragana	Kaisho	Gyoosho	Soosho
WA	わ	和	和	和
O	を	遠	遠	を
N	ん	无	无	ん

カタカナ

なまえ *Namae* (Name) _____

ひづけ *Hizuke* (Date) _____ _____ ようび *Yoobi*
(Day of the week)

Start from the right column. s = stop, t = tail, h = hook.   ↓

お	え	う	い	あ
オ	エ	ウ	イ	ア
オ	エ	ウ	イ	ア
オ	エ	ウ	イ	ア

A **Vertically**

Start here
↓

(Long vowel)			wo		we		wi		ye	
	丨		ウ		ウ		ウ		イ	
			オ		エ		イ		エ	
	丨		ウ		ウ		ウ		イ	
			オ		エ		イ		エ	

B **Horizontally**

Start here
→

ye	イ エ	イ エ					
wi	ウ ィ	ウ ィ					
we	ウ エ	ウ エ					
wo	ウ ォ	ウ ォ					
(Long vowel)	一	一					

A Write the *hiragana* equivalents.

1. オ (　) 　 2. ウ (　) 　 3. エ (　) 　 4. ア (　) 　 5. イ (　)

B The following *katakana* are Chinese last names. Match them with those in the box below.

1. ウーさん (　) 　 2. イーさん (　) 　 3. アウさん (　)

a. Mr. Au	**b.** Mr. Wu	**c.** Mr. Yee

C Choose the *katakana* combinations from the box below which would be used in writing the initial sound of the following words.

1. week (　) 　　 2. walk (　) 　　 3. Wendy (　) 　　 4. whiskey (　)

5. water (　) 　　 6. (Mr.) Yates (　) 　　 7. wedding (　) 　　 8. waiter (　)

a. イエ	**b.** ウィ	**c.** ウエ	**d.** ウォ

D Write the correct *katakana* in the (　).

Use ア/イ/ウ/エ/オ/イェ/ウィ/ウェ/ウォ/ー.

Use ー for long vowel sounds. The small *katakana* occupies its own space.

1. ice 　　(　) 　(　) 　(ス)
　　　　　　　a　　　　i　　　su

2. auto 　(　) 　(　) 　(ト)
　　　　　　o　　　　o　　　to

3. eight 　(　) 　(　) 　(ト)
　　　　　　e　　　　i　　　to

4. week 　(　) 　(　) 　(　) 　(ク)
　　　　　　wi　　　　i　　　　　ku

5. water 　(　) 　(　) 　(　) 　(タ) 　(　)
　　　　　　wo　　　　o　　　　　ta　　　　a

6. waiter 　(　) 　(　) 　(　) 　(タ) 　(　)
　　　　　　we　　　　i　　　　　ta　　　　a

Start from the right column. s = stop, t = tail, h = hook. ↓

こ	け	く	き	か
コ	ケ	ク	キ	カ
	コ	ケ	ク	キ	カ
	コ	ケ	ク	キ	カ

カタカナ KATAKANA

Start from the right column. s = stop, t = tail, h = hook.　　　　↓

ご	げ	ぐ	ぎ	が
ゴ	ゲ	グ	ギ	ガ
ゴ	ゲ	グ	ギ	ガ
ゴ	ゲ	グ	ギ	ガ

A Vertically

Start here
↓

		gwa			kwo			kwa
		グ			ク			ク
		ア			オ			ア
		グ			ク			ク
		ア			オ			ア

B Horizontally

Start here
→

kwa	ク ア	ク ア					
kwo	ク オ	ク オ					
gwa	グ ア	グ ア					

A Write the *hiragana* equivalents.

1. ゲ (　) 　　2. ク (　) 　　3. ケ (　) 　　4. ア (　) 　　5. ギ (　)

6. カ (　) 　　7. ウ (　) 　　8. エ (　) 　　9. オ (　) 　　10. キ (　)

11. コ (　) 　　12. グ (　) 　　13. ゴ (　) 　　14. ガ (　) 　　15. イ (　)

B These are Japanese first names. Find the same names in *hiragana* in the box.
Circle the one name which belongs to a male.

1. アキオ (　) 　　2. アイコ (　) 　　3. エイコ (　) 　　4. ケイコ (　)

a. あいこ　　b. あきお　　c. けいこ　　d. えいこ

C These are Japanese last names. Match them with the same names in *hiragana*.

1. アオキ (　) 　　2. コイケ (　) 　　3. アカイ (　) 　　4. アカイケ (　)

5. アカオ (　) 　　6. ウエキ (　) 　　7. オウエ (　) 　　8. イゲ (　)

a. うえき　　　b. あかい　　c. あおき　　d. あかお
e. あかいけ　　f. こいけ　　g. いげ　　h. おうえ

D Choose the *katakana* combinations from the box below which would be used to write the
underlined portions of the following words.

1. winter (　) 　　2. guava (　) 　　3. waitress (　) 　　4. walk (　)

5. quarter (　) 　　6. Yeltsin (　) 7. iguana (　)

a. イェ　b. ウィ　c. ウェ　d. ウォ　e. クァ　f. クォ　g. グァ

E Complete the following words by writing the correct *katakana* in the parentheses.

1. milk [*miruku*] 　ミル (　)　　　6. U.S. [*amerika*]　　　(　) メリ (　)

2. video [*bideo*] 　ビデ (　)　　　7. garage [*gareeji*]　　(　) レ (　) ジ

3. toilet [*toire*] 　ト (　) レ　　　8. coffee [*koohii*]　　(　) (　) ヒ (　)

4. piano [*piano*] 　ピ (　) ノ　　　9. cafeteria [*kafeteria*]　(　) フェテリ (　)

5. guitar [*gitaa*] 　(　) タ (　)

Start from the right column. s = stop, t = tail, h = hook.
↓

そ	せ	す	し	さ
ソ	セ	ス	シ	サ
	セ	ス	シ	サ
ソ	セ	ス	シ	サ

カタカナ KATAKANA

Start from the right column. s = stop, t = tail, h = hook.   ↓

ぞ	ぜ	ず	じ	ざ
ゾ	ゼ	ズ	ジ	ザ
	ゾ	ゼ	ズ	ジ	ザ
	ゾ	ゼ	ズ	ジ	ザ

A Vertically

Start here

je

she

		ジ			シ
		エ			エ
		ジ			シ
		エ			エ

B Horizontally

Start here →

she シ	エ	シ	エ				
je ジ	エ	ジ	エ				

Ⓐ **Write the *hiragana* equivalents.**

1. グ (   )   2. ズ (   )   3. ケ (   )   4. シ (   )   5. ギ (   )

6. ゾ (   )   7. サ (   )   8. エ (   )   9. ア (   )   10. ス (   )

11. コ (   )   12. ソ (   )   13. ジ (   )   14. セ (   )   15. ゼ (   )

Ⓑ Match **the *hiragana* and *katakana* readings of the following Japanese last names.**

1. アサイ (   )   2. アサオ (   )   3. アカイ (   )   4. サカウエ (   )

5. オオサカ (   )   6. イシイ (   )   7. キシ (   )   8. スガ (   )

9. ソウガ (   )   10. セガ (   )   11. アソウ (   )   12. ウジイエ (   )

a. おおさか	b. あかい	c. うじいえ	d. すが
e. きし	f. あさい	g. せが	h. そうが
i. いしい	j. さかうえ	k. あさお	l. あそう

Ⓒ **Onomatopoetic Expressions: Match the most appropriate English equivalent to each Japanese onomatopoeia by writing the correct letter in the ( ).**

(   ) 1. ザーザー   (   ) 2. グーグー   (   ) 3. エイ!

(   ) 4. キー   (   ) 5. イー!

a. screech

b. shout of attack

c. mocking expression of dislike

d. snoring

e. rain pouring down

D Complete the following words by writing the correct *katakana* in the parentheses.

1. garage [*gareeji*]   (   )レ(   )(   )

2. Spain [*supein*]   (   )ペ(   )ン

3. radio [*rajio*]   ラ(   )(   )

4. orange [*orenji*]   (   )レン(   )

5. taxi [*takushii*]   タ(   )(   )(   )

6. waitress [*weitoresu*]   (   )(   )(   )トレ(   )

7. ice [*aisu*]   (   )(   )(   )

E Identify the *katakana* combinations from the box below which would be used to write the underlined portions of the following words.

1. Jane   (   )   2. guava   (   )   3. waitress   (   )   4. wink   (   )

5. quarter   (   )   6. Yale   (   )   7. water   (   )   8. shake   (   )

a. イェ	b. ウィ	c. ウェ	d. ウォ
e. クォ	f. グァ	g. シェ	h. ジェ

どこですか？

ベルリン

（　　）

マドリッド

（　　）

a. アフリカ
b. アメリカ
c. サウスアメリカ
d. オーストラリア
e. スペイン
f. メキシコ
g. ドイツ

ワシントン D.C.

（　　）

メキシコ
シティ

（　　）

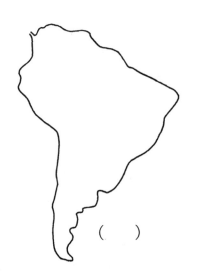

（　　）

（　　）

キャンベラ

（　　）

Start from the right column. s = stop, t = tail, h = hook.   ↓

と	て	っ*	ち	た
ト	テ	ツ	チ	タ
ト	テ	ツ	チ	タ
ト	テ	ツ	チ	タ

カタカナ KATAKANA

* **Compare:** シ (shi) and ツ (tsu). **Also note that a small** ツ **indicates a double consonant, just as in** *hiragana*.

Start from the right column. s = stop, t = tail, h = hook. ↓

ど	で	(づ)*	ぢ*	だ
ド	デ	ツ	ヂ	ダ
	ド	デ	ヅ	ヂ	ダ
	ド	デ	ヅ	ヂ	ダ

*These *katakana* are rarely used.

Start here
↓

A Vertically

	di	ti	tso	tse	tsa	che
	デ	テ	ツ	ツ	ツ	チ
	イ	イ	オ	エ	ア	エ
	デ	テ	ツ	ツ	ツ	チ
	イ	イ	オ	エ	ア	エ

カタカナ   KATAKANA

B Horizontally

Start here
→

che	チェ	チェ								
tsa	ツァ	ツァ								
tse	ツェ	ツェ								
tso	ツォ	ツォ								
ti	ティ	ティ								
di	ディ	ディ								

A Write the *hiragana* equivalents.

1. テ （　）　　　2. ゾ （　）　　　3. ケ （　）　　　4. タ （　）　　　5. シ （　）

6. ド （　）　　　7. ウ （　）　　　8. ト （　）　　　9. オ （　）　　　10. デ （　）

11. ズ （　）　　　12. グ （　）　　　13. チ （　）　　　14. サ （　）　　　15. ツ （　）

B Match the *katakana* and *hiragana* readings of the following Japanese last names.

1. アキタ （　）　　2. アシダ （　）　　3. タオカ （　）　　4. ウエダ （　）

5. オカダ （　）　　6. オキタ （　）　　7. タケダ （　）　　8. サカタ （　）

9. イシダ （　）　　10. ダテ （　）　　11. ドイ （　）　　12. タキシタ （　）

a. おかだ	b. たおか	c. いしだ	d. さかた
e. あしだ	f. うえだ	g. だて	h. たけだ
i. あきた	j. おきた	k. どい	l. たきした

C Match the *katakana* names with their English equivalents.

1. スー （　）　　　　2. スージー （　）　3. ジェシカ （　）　4. ケーシー （　）

5. ダック or ドック （　）　6. アート （　）　　7. ジェシー （　）

8. タッド or トッド （　）　9. ディック （　）　10. ティー （　）

a. Doc	**b.** Todd	**c.** Suzie	**d.** Art
e. Jessica	**f.** Sue	**g.** Jessie	**h.** Tee
i. Dick	**j.** Casey		

D Read the following *katakana* words. Then write their English equivalents. Use the cues in the brackets.

English　　　　　　　　　　　　　　　　　　　　　　　English

1. チェリー [fruit]　_____　　5. フォーク [utensil]　_____

2. ディック [name]　_____　　6. ディナー [meal]　_____

3. アイスティー [drink]　_____　　7. ティーシャツ [clothing]　_____

4. キャンディー [sweet]　_____　　8. チェス [game]　_____

E **Onomatopoetic Expressions: Match the most appropriate English equivalent to each Japanese onomatopoeia by writing the correct letter in the ( ).**

( ) 1. シー

( ) 2. カッカ

( ) 3. コケコッコー

( ) 4. ドキドキ

a. heart pounding
b. shhh!
c. cockle doodle doo!
d. fuming with anger

F **Complete the following words.**

1. video [*bideo*]　　　　　ビ（　）（　）

2. Spain [*supein*]　　　　（　）ペ（　）ン

3. chocolate [*chokoreeto*]　チョ（　）レ（　）（　）

4. Canada [*kanada*]　　　（　）ナ（　）

5. taxi [*takushii*]　　　　（　）（　）（　）（　）

6. Germany [*doitsu*]　　　（　）（　）（　）

7. computer [*konpyuutaa*]　（　）ンピュ（　）（　）（　）

8. toilet [*toire*]　　　　　（　）（　）レ

9. guitar [*gitaa*]　　　　　（　）（　）（　）

KATAKANA

カタカナ

なんのスポーツですか？

 ( )

 ( )

 ( )

 ( )

 ( )

a. テニス
b. スイミング
c. スキー
d. ジョギング
e. ゴルフ
f. サッカー
g. フットボール
h. バスケットボール
i. ベースボール
j. バレーボール
k. ランニング

 ( )

 ( )

 ( )

 ( )

 ( )

Start from the right column. s = stop, t = tail, h = hook.   ↓

の		ね		ぬ		に		な	
ノ		ネ		ヌ		ニ		ナ	
	ノ		ネ		ヌ		ニ		ナ
	ノ		ネ		ヌ		ニ		ナ

KATAKANA カタカナ

A Write the *hiragana* equivalents.

1. ニ (　　) 　 2. ツ (　　) 　 3. ネ (　　) 　 4. テ (　　) 　 5. ヌ (　　)

6. ス (　　) 　 7. ケ (　　) 　 8. ウ (　　) 　 9. ノ (　　) 　 10. サ (　　)

11. タ (　　) 　 12. ナ (　　) 　 13. ト (　　) 　 14. オ (　　) 　 15. チ (　　)

16. イ (　　) 　 17. ア (　　) 　 18. エ (　　) 　 19. ソ (　　) 　 20. キ (　　)

21. ク (　　) 　 22. カ (　　) 　 23. シ (　　) 　 24. コ (　　) 　 25. セ (　　)

B Match the *katakana* names with their English equivalents.

1. ジーナ (　　) 　 2. ジェニー (　　) 　 3. ジニー (　　) 　 4. ケニー (　　)

5. トニー (　　) 　 6. ダニー (　　) 　 7. シドニー (　　) 8. ネッド (　　)

a. Kenny	**b.** Ginny	**c.** Gina	**d.** Danny
e. Jenny	**f.** Sydney	**g.** Ned	**h.** Tony

C Write the English equivalents of the *katakana* words below. Use the cues given in [ ].

English

1. カヌー [sport] _____

2. ソニー [company] _____

3. ディナー [meal] _____

4. ノート [stationery] _____

5. スキー [sport] _____

6. スケート [sport] _____

English

7. スノーケル [sport] _____

8. カップヌードル [food] _____

9. スノーボード [sport] _____

10. スナックバー [place] _____

11. セイコー [company] _____

12. テニス [sport] _____

D Circle the English term that best matches the drawing and onomatopoetic expression.

ニコニコ

a. uncontrolled laughter
b. hearty laughter
c. polite laughter
d. smiling

Start from the right column. s = stop, t = tail, h = hook.   ↓

ほ	へ	ふ	ひ	は
ホ	ヘ	フ	ヒ	ハ
ホ	ヘ	フ	ヒ	ハ
ホ	ヘ	フ	ヒ	ハ

Start from the right column. s = stop, t = tail, h = hook. ↓

ぼ		べ		ぶ		び		ば
ボ		ベ		ブ		ビ		バ
	ボ		ベ		ブ		ビ	バ
	ボ		ベ		ブ		ビ	バ

Start from the right column. s = stop, t = tail, h = hook.   ↓

ぽ	ぺ	ぷ	ぴ	ぱ
ポ	ペ	プ	ピ	パ
ポ	ペ	プ	ピ	パ
ポ	ペ	プ	ピ	パ

カタカナ　KATAKANA

A **Vertically**

Start here
↓

	fo		fe		fi		fa
	フ		フ		フ		フ
	オ		エ		イ		ア
	フ		フ		フ		フ
	オ		エ		イ		ア

B **Horizontally**

Start here
→

fa	フ	ァ	フ	ァ				
fi	フ	ィ	フ	ィ				
fe	フ	エ	フ	エ				
fo	フ	ォ	フ	ォ				

A Write the *hiragana* equivalents.

1. ヒ ( )　　2. チ ( )　　3. ツ ( )　　4. バ ( )　　5. ヘ ( )

6. ブ ( )　　7. ノ ( )　　8. ビ ( )　　9. テ ( )　　10. ポ ( )

11. ホ ( )　　12. ハ ( )　　13. シ ( )　　14. ペ ( )　　15. フ ( )

16. ヌ ( )　　17. ト ( )　　18. サ ( )　　19. ソ ( )　　20. ネ ( )

21. ナ ( )　　22. ニ ( )　　23. オ ( )　　24. ス ( )　　25. タ ( )

B Match the *katakana* readings with the English names.

1. ハイジ ( )　　2. ボブ ( )　　3. ピーター ( )　　4. フランク ( )

5. ベッキー ( )　　6. ベン ( )　　7. ポール ( )　　8. ポーラ ( )

a. Bob	b. Frank	c. Paula	d. Becky
e. Ben	f. Heidi	g. Paul	h. Peter

C Write the English equivalents. Use the cues given in brackets.

English

1. ポップコーン [food] _____

2. フォーク [utensil] _____

3. カフェテリア [place] _____

4. フィッシング [sport] _____

5. フォト [thing] _____

6. フェンシング [sport] _____

English

7. ボールペン [thing] _____

8. ピーナッツ [food] _____

9. フィンランド [country] _____

10. ドーナツ [food] _____

11. ピンポン [sport] _____

12. フィラデルフィア [city] _____

カタカナ　KATAKANA

D Onomatopoetic Expressions: Match the most appropriate English equivalent to each Japanese onomatopoeia by writing the correct letter in the ( ).

( ) 1. ブーブー

( ) 2. ピーピー

( ) 3. ピカピカ

( ) 4. フーフー

( ) 5. パチパチ

( ) 6. パクパク

a. crackling, clapping	**b.** chirping	**c.** forceful blowing
d. mouth-smacking, gobbling down food	**e.** oink, oink	**f.** shining, sparkling

E Write the following words in *katakan*a.

1. piano [*piano*]　　　　( ) ( ) ( )

2. coffee [*koohii*]　　　( ) ( ) ( ) ( )

3. video [*bideo*]　　　　( ) ( ) ( )

4. Spain [*supein*]　　　( ) ( ) ( ) ン

5. cafeteria [*kafeteria*]　( ) ( ) ( ) ( ) リ ( )

6. picnic [*pikunikku*]　　( ) ( ) ( ) ( ) ( )

7. pink [*pinku*]　　　　( ) ン ( )

8. golf [*gorufu*]　　　　( ) ル ( )

9. party [*paatii*]　　　( ) ( ) ( ) ( ) ( )

10. sports [*supootsu*]　　( ) ( ) ( ) ( )

Start from the right column. s = stop, t = tail, h = hook. ↓

も	め	む	み	ま
モ	メ	ム	ミ	マ
モ	メ	ム	ミ	マ
モ	メ	ム	ミ	マ

A Write the *hiragana* equivalents.

1. ヌ (　) 　2. ミ (　) 　3. ゾ (　) 　4. メ (　) 　5. ビ (　)

6. バ (　) 　7. チ (　) 　8. ノ (　) 　9. ス (　) 　10. ツ (　)

11. テ (　) 　12. プ (　) 　13. マ (　) 　14. セ (　) 　15. モ (　)

16. ム (　) 　17. ク (　) 　18. エ (　) 　19. タ (　) 　20. シ (　)

21. ゴ (　) 　22. ネ (　) 　23. ト (　) 　24. ポ (　) 　25. ナ (　)

B Match the *katakana* names with their English equivalents.

1. マリー (　) 　　2. ミリー (　) 　　3. タミー (　) 　　4. キム (　)

5. ティム (　) 　　6. マドンナ (　) 　7. トム (　) 　　8. ジミー (　)

9. メリー (　) 　　10. マイク (　) 　　11. ミッキー (　) 　12. エミー (　)

13. エミリー (　) 　14. ジム (　) 　　15. モリス (　) 　　16. マック (　)

a. Kim	**b.** Tom	**c.** Tim	**d.** Jimmy
e. Marie	**f.** Emily	**g.** Amy	**h.** Morris
i. Tammy	**j.** Jim	**k.** Millie	**l.** Mike
m. Mac	**n.** Mary	**o.** Madonna	**p.** Mickey

C Write the English equivalents. Use the hints given in brackets.

English　　　　　　　　　　　　　　　　English

1. ハム [food] _____　　8. ミルク [drink] _____

2. ガム [snack] _____　　9. ビール [drink] _____

3. ホットドッグ [food] _____　　10. ペプシコーラ [drink] _____

4. ハンバーガー [food] _____　　11. マクドナルド [place] _____

5. ピザ [food] _____　　12. アイスクリーム [food] _____

6. スパゲッティ [food] _____　　13. モーツァルト [composer] _____

7. パンケーキ [food] _____　　14. ストロベリー [food] _____

D Onomatopoetic Expressions: Match the most appropriate English equivalent to each Japanese onomatopoeia by writing the correct letter in the ( ).

( ) 1. モー

( ) 2. ガミガミ

( ) 3. メソメソ

( ) 4. モシモシ

a. nagging, scolding

b. moo

c. whimper, sniffle

d. phone greeting

E Write the *katakana* equivalents of the following words.

1. U.S. [*amerika*]   (   ) (   ) リ (   )

2. milk [*miruku*]   (   ) ル (   )

3. picnic [*pikunikku*]   (   ) (   ) (   ) ( ) (   )

なんのベジタブル？　　なんのフルーツ？

 （　　）　　 （　　）　　 （　　）　　 （　　）

 （　　）

あ．　バナナ
い．　アップル
う．　ポテト
え．　グレープ
お．　レタス
か．　パイナップル
き．　オニオン
く．　セロリ
け．　ストロベリー
こ．　トマト
さ．　メロン
し．　ピーチ
す．　オレンジ
せ．　キャロット
そ．　チェリー

 （　　）

 （　　）

 （　　）

 （　　）

 （　　）

 （　　）　　 （　　）　　 （　　）　　 （　　）　　 （　　）

Start from the right column. s = stop, t = tail, h = hook.   ↓

	よ			ゆ			や
	ヨ			ユ			ヤ
	ヨ			ユ			ヤ
	ヨ			ユ			ヤ

カタカナ KATAKANA

A **Vertically**

Start here ↓

hyo	hyu	hya	nyo	nyu	nya	cho	chu	cha	sho	shu	sha	kyo	kyu	kya
ヒ	ヒ	ヒ	ニ	ニ	ニ	チ	チ	チ	シ	シ	シ	キ	キ	キ
ヨ	ユ	ヤ	ヨ	ユ	ヤ	ヨ	ユ	ヤ	ヨ	ユ	ヤ	ヨ	ユ	ヤ
ヒ	ヒ	ヒ	ニ	ニ	ニ	チ	チ	チ	シ	シ	シ	キ	キ	キ
ヨ	ユ	ヤ	ヨ	ユ	ヤ	ヨ	ユ	ヤ	ヨ	ユ	ヤ	ヨ	ユ	ヤ

pyo	pyu	pya	byo	byu	bya	jo	ju	ja	gyo	gyu	gya	myo	myu	mya
ピ	ピ	ピ	ビ	ビ	ビ	ジ	ジ	ジ	ギ	ギ	ギ	ミ	ミ	ミ
ヨ	ユ	ヤ	ヨ	ユ	ヤ	ヨ	ユ	ヤ	ヨ	ユ	ヤ	ヨ	ユ	ヤ
ピ	ピ	ピ	ビ	ビ	ビ	ジ	ジ	ジ	ギ	ギ	ギ	ミ	ミ	ミ
ヨ	ユ	ヤ	ヨ	ユ	ヤ	ヨ	ユ	ヤ	ヨ	ユ	ヤ	ヨ	ユ	ヤ

B **Horizontally**

Start here →   →

kya	キ	ャ	キ	ャ		
kyu	キ	ュ	キ	ュ		
kyo	キ	ョ	キ	ョ		
sha	シ	ャ	シ	ャ		
shu	シ	ュ	シ	ュ		
sho	シ	ョ	シ	ョ		
cha	チ	ャ	チ	ャ		
chu	チ	ュ	チ	ュ		
cho	チ	ョ	チ	ョ		
nya	ニ	ャ	ニ	ャ		
nyu	ニ	ュ	ニ	ュ		
nyo	ニ	ョ	ニ	ョ		
hya	ヒ	ャ	ヒ	ャ		
hyu	ヒ	ュ	ヒ	ュ		
hyo	ヒ	ョ	ヒ	ョ		

mya	ミ	ャ	ミ	ャ		
myu	ミ	ュ	ミ	ュ		
myo	ミ	ョ	ミ	ョ		
gya	ギ	ャ	ギ	ャ		
gyu	ギ	ュ	ギ	ュ		
gyo	ギ	ョ	ギ	ョ		
ja	ジ	ャ	ジ	ャ		
ju	ジ	ュ	ジ	ュ		
jo	ジ	ョ	ジ	ョ		
bya	ビ	ャ	ビ	ャ		
byu	ビ	ュ	ビ	ュ		
byo	ビ	ョ	ビ	ョ		
pya	ピ	ャ	ピ	ャ		
pyu	ピ	ュ	ピ	ュ		
pyo	ピ	ョ	ピ	ョ		

A Write the *hiragana* equivalents.

1. ム（　　） 　　2. ニ（　　） 　　3. モ（　　） 　　4. フ（　　） 　　5. ヤ（　　）

6. ヌ（　　） 　　7. ノ（　　） 　　8. マ（　　） 　　9. ナ（　　） 　　10. チ（　　）

11. ホ（　　） 　12. ヒ（　　） 　13. シ（　　） 　14. ユ（　　） 　15. ソ（　　）

16. ミ（　　） 　17. テ（　　） 　18. ト（　　） 　19. ネ（　　） 　20. ヘ（　　）

21. ツ（　　） 　22. メ（　　） 　23. ヨ（　　） 　24. ハ（　　） 　25. タ（　　）

B Match the *katakana* names with their English equivalents.

1. ジョイ（　　） 　　2. ジョージ（　　） 　3. ジャッキー（　　） 　4. ジュリー（　　）

5. ジュディー（　　） 　6. ショーン（　　） 　7. ジェフ（　　） 　　8. ジョン（　　）

9. ギャビン（　　） 　10. ケシャ（　　） 　11. ミッシェル（　　） 　12. ジェシカ（　　）

13. ユーニス（　　） 　14. キャシー（　　） 　15. チャーリー（　　） 　16. ジョシュア（　　）

a. Gavin	**b.** Jackie	**c.** Eunice	**d.** Cathy
e. Jon	**f.** Judy	**g.** Julie	**h.** Charlie
i. Joy	**j.** Jeff	**k.** Sean	**l.** Joshua
m. Jessica	**n.** Kesha	**o.** Michelle	**p.** George

C Here are some baseball terms in *katakana*. Guess what they are in English.

English

1. ベースボール　_____

2. キャッチャー　_____

3. ピッチャー　_____

4. コーチ　_____

5. マネージャー　_____

6. バット　_____

7. グローブ　_____

8. ストライク　_____

English

9. ボール　_____

10. ファウル　_____

11. アウト　_____

12. セーフ　_____

13. スチール　_____

14. ホームラン　_____

15. アンパイヤー　_____

16. スコアー　_____

D Onomatopoetic Expressions: Match the most appropriate English equivalent to each Japanese onomatopoeia by writing the correct letter in the ( ).

( ) 1. チューチュー   ( ) 2. ペチャクチャ   ( ) 3. オギャーオギャー

( ) 4. チュッ   ( ) 5. ヤッター   ( ) 6. キャー!

( ) 7. メチャクチャ

a. eek!
b. squeak!
c. smack! (kiss)
d. messy
e. yay!
f. baby's cry
g. chatter

E Write the following words in *katakana*.

1. computer [*konpyuutaa*]   ( ) ン ( ) ( ) ( ) ( ) ( )

2. chocolate [*chokoreeto*]   ( ) ( ) ( ) レ ( ) ( )

3. jogging [*jogingu*]   ( ) ( ) ( ) ン ( )

4. juice [*juusu*]   ( ) ( ) ( ) ( )

カタカナ KATAKANA

なんですか？

 ( )
 ( )
 ( )
 ( )

あ. ホットドッグ
い. ミルク
う. ジュース
え. サンドイッチ
お. ナイフ
か. ピザ
き. フォーク
く. フライドポテト
け. コーラ
こ. スプーン
さ. コップ
し. コーヒー
す. ハンバーガー
せ. チョコレート
そ. ナプキン
た. ストロー

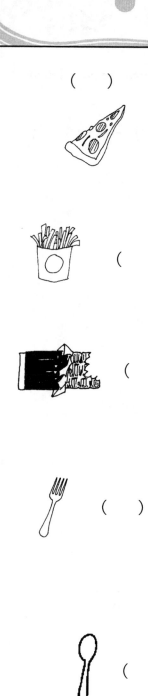 ( )

( )

( )

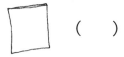 ( )

( )

( )

 ( )

 ( )

 ( )

 ( )

Start from the right column. s = stop, t = tail, h = hook.   ↓

ろ	れ	る	り	ら
ロ	レ	ル	リ	ラ
ロ	レ	ル	リ	ラ
ロ	レ	ル	リ	ラ

A **Vertically**

Start here
↓

		ryo			ryu			rya
		リ			リ			リ
		ヨ			ユ			ヤ
		リ			リ			リ
		ヨ			ユ			ヤ

B **Horizontally**

Start here
→

rya	リ	ヤ	リ	ヤ					
ryu	リ	ユ	リ	ユ					
ryo	リ	ヨ	リ	ヨ					

A **Write the *hiragana* equivalents.**

1. ハ (　　) 2. レ (　　) 3. モ (　　) 4. ヤ (　　) 5. ロ (　　)

6. ヨ (　　) 7. ム (　　) 8. ネ (　　) 9. ホ (　　) 10. ノ (　　)

11. フ (　　) 12. マ (　　) 13. ラ (　　) 14. ツ (　　) 15. ユ (　　)

16. ナ (　　) 17. ヌ (　　) 18. ス (　　) 19. リ (　　) 20. チ (　　)

21. ル (　　) 22. ヒ (　　) 23. メ (　　) 24. ト (　　) 25. ミ (　　)

26. オ (　　) 27. ク (　　) 28. ウ (　　) 29. コ (　　) 30. ア (　　)

B **Match the *katakana* names with their English equivalents.**

1. キャラ (　　) 2. レスリー (　　) 3. ウィリー (　　) 4. アレン (　　)

5. ドーラ (　　) 6. ローリー (　　) 7. ケリー (　　) 8. テリー (　　)

9. ノラ (　　) 10. リッキー (　　) 11. サリー (　　) 12. レイチェル (　　)

13. ハリー (　　) 14. ネリー (　　) 15. クリス (　　) 16. マリー (　　)

17. リック (　　) 18. ライアン (　　) 19. ビル (　　) 20. アンディー (　　)

a. Nora	**b.** Nellie	**c.** Rick	**d.** Rachel
e. Alan	**f.** Dora	**g.** Marie	**h.** Ricky
i. Cara	**j.** Harry	**k.** Sally	**l.** Bill
m. Andy	**n.** Chris	**o.** Leslie	**p.** Terry
q. Ryan	**r.** Lori	**s.** Kelly	**t.** Willy

C **Many computer terms are written in *katakana*.**
Guess what these are in English.

English

1. プリンター _____
2. スクリーン _____
3. イーメール _____
4. マウス _____
5. パソコン _____

English

6. マニュアル _____
7. プログラム _____
8. ファイル _____
9. グラフィック _____
10. ダブルクリック _____

カタカナ　KATAKANA

D **Onomatopoetic Expressions: Match the most appropriate English equivalent to each Japanese onomatopoeia by writing the correct letter in the ( ).**

( ) 1. ボロボロ

( ) 2. ガッカリ

( ) 3. クルクルパー

( ) 4. コラッ!

> **a.** hey! (scolding)
>
> **b.** disappointment
>
> **c.** ragged, worn
>
> **d.** crazy!

E **Write the following words in *katakana*.**

1. U.S. [*amerika*]　　　( ) ( ) ( ) ( )

2. radio [*rajio*]　　　( ) ( ) ( )

3. chocolate [*chokoreeto*]　　　( ) ( ) ( ) ( ) ( ) ( )

4. milk [*miruku*]　　　( ) ( ) ( )

5. cola [*koora*]　　　( ) ( ) ( )

6. cafeteria [*kafeteria*]　　　( ) ( ) ( ) ( ) ( ) ( )

7. toilet [*toire*]　　　( ) ( ) ( )

8. locker [*rokkaa*]　　　( ) ( ) ( ) ( )

9. ballpoint pen [*boorupen*]　　　( ) ( ) ( ) ( ) ン

10. orange [*orenji*]　　　( ) ( ) ン ( )

11. TV [*terebi*]　　　( ) ( ) ( )

12. golf [*gorufu*]　　　( ) ( ) ( )

Start from the right column. s = stop, t = tail, h = hook.   ↓

	ん			を			わ
	ン			ヲ			ワ
	ン			ヲ			ワ
	ン			ヲ			ワ

カタカナ KATAKANA

Compare: ソ "SO" and ン "N", ワ "WA" and ク "KU"

なまえ *Namae* (Name) _____

ひづけ *Hizuke* (Date) _____ _____ ようび *Yoobi*
(Day of the week)

Ⓐ Write the *hiragana* equivalents.

1. ン (　) 　　2. ソ (　) 　　3. シ (　) 　　4. ツ (　) 　　5. タ (　)

6. ク (　) 　　7. ネ (　) 　　8. ワ (　) 　　9. ウ (　) 　　10. コ (　)

11. ユ (　) 　12. テ (　) 　13. ノ (　) 　14. メ (　) 　15. ナ (　)

16. フ (　) 　17. ラ (　) 　18. マ (　) 　19. ム (　) 　20. ヤ (　)

21. セ (　) 　22. ロ (　) 　23. ヨ (　) 　24. レ (　) 　25. ル (　)

26. ア (　) 　27. オ (　) 　28. イ (　) 　29. ケ (　) 　30. サ (　)

Ⓑ Match the *katakana* names with their English equivalents.

1. ジョン (　) 　　2. リン (　) 　　3. リンダ (　) 　　4. マリアン (　)

5. ベン (　) 　　6. ジョアン (　) 　7. ジェイン (　) 　8. リリアン (　)

9. ケン (　) 　10. イレイン (　) 　11. ダン (　) 　12. キャレン (　)

13. アン (　) 　14. ダイアン (　) 　15. ヘレン (　) 　16. ダレン (　)

a. Ken	**b.** Darren	**c.** Lynn	**d.** Ben
e. Diane	**f.** John	**g.** Elaine	**h.** Karen
i. Ann	**j.** Dan	**k.** Lillian	**l.** Marian
m. Helen	**n.** Joann	**o.** Jane	**p.** Linda

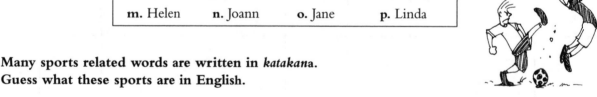

**Ⓒ Many sports related words are written in *katakana*.
Guess what these sports are in English.**

　　　　　　　　　　English　　　　　　　　　　　　　　　　　English

1. レスリング 　_____ 　6. マラソン 　_____

2. ピンポン 　_____ 　7. ダイビング 　_____

3. ソフトボール 　_____ 　8. サーフィン 　_____

4. アイスホッケー 　_____ 　9. スイミング 　_____

5. ジョギング 　_____ 　10. サッカー 　_____

D **Onomatopoetic Expressions: Match the most appropriate English equivalent to each Japanese onomatopoeia by writing the correct letter in the ( ).**

( ) 1. ニヤーンニャーン   ( ) 2. ワンワン   ( ) 3. プンプン

( ) 4. ハクション   ( ) 5. ゴホンゴホン   ( ) 6. ワッハッハ

a. ahchoo!	**d.** arf, arf! (barking)
b. meow!	**e.** raging anger
c. ha, ha, ha (hearty laughter)	**f.** cough, cough!

E **Complete the following words in *katakan*a.**

1. France [*furansu*]   ( ) ( ) ( ) ( )

2. Spain [*supein*]   ( ) ( ) ( ) ( )

3. camp [*kyanpu*]   ( ) ( ) ( ) ( )

4. computer [*konpyuutaa*]   ( ) ( ) ( ) ( ) ( ) ( )

5. pink [*pinku*]   ( ) ( ) ( )

6. orange [*orenji*]   ( ) ( ) ( ) ( )

7. dance [*dansu*]   ( ) ( ) ( )

KATAKANA カタカナ

A Vertically

Start here
↓

	vyu		vo		ve		vi		va
	ヴ		ヴ		ヴ		ヴ		ヴ
	ユ		オ		エ		イ		ア
	ヴ		ヴ		ヴ		ヴ		ヴ
	ユ		オ		エ		イ		ア

B Horizontally

Start here
→

va	ヴ	ァ	ヴ	ァ						
vi	ヴ	ィ	ヴ	ィ						
ve	ヴ	エ	ヴ	エ						
vo	ヴ	オ	ヴ	オ						
vyu	ヴ	ユ	ヴ	ユ						

C What are these musical instruments? Write the answers in English.

1. ヴァイオリン _____

2. ヴィオラ _____

漢字

Guide to Writing Kanji

Like *hiragana* and *katakana*, *kanji* are written in a series of strokes, although the number of strokes is often much greater. It is important to follow the correct stroke order so you can write faster and in better form. It will also help you use computers with Japanese handwriting recognition software.

How to Write Strokes

Most individual strokes are written in one of two simple directions.

Horizontal strokes go from left to right　　　*Vertical strokes go from top to bottom*

The end of a stroke is also important. There are three ways to finish a stroke:

a blunt stop ⌐　　a hook ↳　　a tail ⌴

The way each stroke ends is clear when *kanji* is written with a brush, but not as obvious when written with a pen or a pencil, or in some digital fonts.

Basic Stroke Order

The order of strokes in *kanji* follows seven basic patterns.

 1. Top strokes before lower strokes

 2. Left strokes before right strokes

 3. Center strokes before outside strokes

 4. Strokes connecting to other strokes first

 5. Strokes passing through other strokes last

 6. Make the outside frame first, then fill the inside, then close

 7. Right-to-left diagonals before left-to-right diagonals

名前 _____

日づけ _____ _____ 曜日

A Practice writing the new *kanji*.

Write each *kanji* by first tracing each stroke in the correct order shown below. Complete all of the boxes by writing the entire *kanji* in the correct order in each box.

1	一 one	いち ひと(つ)	いち 一 one いち 一まい one (flat objects)	ひと 一つ one (general objects) ついたち *一日 first day of the month

一 一 _ _ _ _ _ _ _ _

一 一 一 _ _ _ _ _ _ _

2	二 two	に ふた(つ)	に 二 two に 二まい two (flat objects)	ふた 二つ two (general objects) ふっか *二か second day of the month

二 二 _ _ _ _ _ _ _ _

二 二 二 _ _ _ _ _ _ _

3	三 three	さん みっ(つ)	さん 三 three さん 三まい three (flat objects)	さんにん 三人 three (people) みっ 三つ three (general objects)

三 三 三 _ _ _ _ _ _ _

三 三 三 _ _ _ _ _ _ _

4	四 four	し よ よん よっ(つ)	よん し 四 or 四 four よ にん 四人 four (people) よん 四まい four (flat objects)	よっ 四つ four (general objects) しがつ 四月 April よっか *四日 fourth day of the month

四 四 四 四 四 _ _ _ _ _

四 四 四 _ _ _ _ _ _ _

NOTE: Irregular pronunciations are marked with a ✱.

漢字 KANJI

| 5 | 五
five | ご
いつ(つ) | ご
五 five
ご
五まい five (flat objects) | ごにん
五人 five (people)
いつ
五つ five (general objects) |

五 五 五 五

五 五 五

| 6 | 日
sun,
day | に
にち
ひ
び
か | にほん
日本 Japan
なんにち
何日 What day of the month?
ひ
日づけ date
なんようび
何曜日 What day of the week?
にちようび
日曜日 Sunday | ふつか
二日 2nd day of the month
みっか
三日 3rd day of the month
よっか
四日 4th day of the month
いつか
五日 5th day of the month
ついたち
*一日 1st day of the month |

日 日 日 日

日 日 日

| **Recognition Kanji**
Name | 名前 | なまえ
名前 name |

B **Match each of the English words in the chart below with the letter of the corresponding illustration and the number of the corresponding *kanji* character.**

Example: one	two	three	four	five	sun, day
d					
3					

| a. | b. | c. | d. | e. | f. |

1. 三 2. 日 3. 一 4. 五 5. 二 6. 四

A Circle the correct readings of the *kanji*.

Ex. 一つ （**ひとつ** ふたつ みっつ よっつ いつつ）

1. 四つ （ひとつ ふたつ みっつ よっつ いつつ）

2. 二つ （ひとつ ふたつ みっつ よっつ いつつ）

3. 五つ （ひとつ ふたつ みっつ よっつ いつつ）

4. 三つ （ひとつ ふたつ みっつ よっつ いつつ）

5. 二日 （ついたち ふつか みっか よっか いつか）

6. 三日 （ついたち ふつか みっか よっか いつか）

7. 五日 （ついたち ふつか みっか よっか いつか）

8. 一日 （ついたち ふつか みっか よっか いつか）

9. 四日 （ついたち ふつか みっか よっか いつか）

10. なん日 （なんに なんにち なんひ なんび なんか）

B Write the correct counters in *hiragana* and *kanji* for the English translations below.

	Hiragana	Kanji
Ex. 5th day of the month	いつか	五日
1. one (general objects)		
2. 3rd day of the month		
3. four (flat objects)		
4. two (general objects)		
5. 1st day of the month		

C Write correct *kanji* in the box and the correct *hiragana* (or *roomaji*) readings in the (   ).

1. 1日 = ☐ 日 = (　)(　)(　)(　)

2. 2日 = ☐ 日 = (　)(　)(　)

3. 3日 = ☐ 日 = (　)つ(　)

4. 4日 = ☐ 日 = (　)つ(　)

5. 5日 = ☐ 日 = (　)(　)(　)

6. 1つ = ☐ つ = (　)(　)(　)

7. 2つ = ☐ つ = (　)(　)(　)

8. 3つ = ☐ つ = (　)つ(　)

Sun	Mon	Tue	Wed	Th
1	2	3	4	5

D Write the correct *kanji* for the underlined *hiragana* in the boxes below. Write the correct readings of the underlined *kanji* in *hiragana* (or *roomaji*) in the (   ).

1. 今日（きょう）は <u>みっか</u>ですか。

☐☐

2. 今日（きょう）は <u>いつか</u>です。

☐☐

3. 今日（きょう）は <u>にち</u>曜（よう）びです。

☐☐

4. 私（わたし）の <u>名前</u>はけんです。

(　　　　)

5. <u>日本</u>（ほん）です。

(　　　　)

6. あめを<u>一つ</u>ください。

(　　　　)

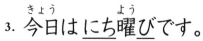

216　Adventures in Japanese 1 • 3か　Family

A Practice writing the new *kanji*.

Write each *kanji* by first tracing each stroke in the correct order shown below. Complete all of the boxes by writing the entire *kanji* in the correct order in each box.

7	六 six	ろく むっ(つ)	ろく 六 six むっ 六つ six (general objects)				むいか *六日 6th day of the month		
			六	六	六	六			
			六	六	六				

8	七 seven	しち なな(つ)	しち 七 seven なな 七つ seven (general objects)			なのか *七日 7th day of the month		
			七	七				
			七	七	七			

9	八 eight	はち やっ(つ)	はち 八 eight やっ 八つ eight (general objects)			ようか *八日 8th day of the month		
			八	八				
			八	八	八			

10	九 nine	きゅう く ここの (つ)	きゅう 九 nine ここの 九つ nine (general objects)			ここのか 九 日 9th day of the month くじ 九時 nine o'clock		
			九	九				
			九	九	九			

NOTE: Irregular pronunciations are marked with a **✳**.

11	十 ten	じゅう とお	じゅう 十　　ten とお 十　　ten (general objects)		とおか 十日　10th day of the month

十	十									
十	十									

12	月 moon, month	がつ げつ つき	いちがつ 一 月　January にがつ 二 月　Feburuary ろくがつ 六 月　June しちがつ 七 月　July	じゅうにがつ 十 二 月　December げつようび 月 曜 日　Monday つき 月　　Moon

月	月	月	月							
月	月	月								

Recognition **Kanji** Tomorrow	明日	あした 明日　tomorrow

B Match each of the English words in the chart below with the letter of the corresponding illustration and the number of the corresponding *kanji* character.

Example: sun	six	seven	eight	nine	ten	moon, month
a						
1						

a.   b.   c.   d.   e.   f.   g.

1. 日   2. 月   3. 九   4. 八   5. 十   6. 七   7. 六

A Circle the correct readings of the *kanji*.

Ex. 一つ （(**ひとつ**)　ふたつ　みっつ　よっつ　いつつ）

1. 八つ （むっつ　ななつ　やっつ　ここのつ　とお）

2. 七つ （むっつ　ななつ　やっつ　ここのつ　とお）

3. 十 （むっつ　ななつ　やっつ　ここのつ　とお）

4. 九つ （むっつ　ななつ　やっつ　ここのつ　とお）

5. 八日 （むいか　なのか　ようか　ここのか　とおか）

6. 十日 （むいか　なのか　ようか　ここのか　とおか）

7. 九日 （むいか　なのか　ようか　ここのか　とおか）

8. 六日 （むいか　なのか　ようか　ここのか　とおか）

9. 七月 （いちがつ　しがつ　しちがつ　くがつ）

10. 九月 （いちがつ　しがつ　しちがつ　くがつ）

11. 月曜日 （にちようび　げつようび　かようび　すいようび　どようび）

12. 明日 （かんじ　にほん　なまえ　あした　ひづけ）

B Write the dates in English.

Ex. 五月二日 _____

1. 八月七日 _____

2. 六月三十日 _____

3. 十月二十五日 _____

4. 九月十七日 _____

5. 十二月六日 _____

6. 七月四日 _____

漢字　Kanji　**219**

C Write the correct dates in *kanji* in the boxes, then write the readings of the dates in *hiragana* or *roomaji* in the (   ).

Ex. January 2

一	月	二	日

(　いちがつ　ふつか　)

1. August 9

(　　　　　　　　　　)

2. May 7

(　　　　　　　　　　)

3. September 6

(　　　　　　　　　　)

4. November 3

(　　　　　　　　　　)

5. April 19

(　　　　　　　　　　)

6. March 20

(　　　　　　　　　　)

D Write the correct *kanji* for the underlined *hiragana* in the boxes below. Write the correct readings of the underlined *kanji* in *hiragana* (or *roomaji*) in the (   ).

1. 今日は　<u>じゅうがつ</u>　<u>むいか</u>です。

2. 明日は　<u>げつ</u>曜びです。

(　　　　　)

3. 今日は　<u>にち</u>曜びです。

4. あめを　<u>とお</u>　ください。

5. ぼくの　<u>名前</u>は　けんです。たんじょう日は　<u>くがつ</u>　<u>はつか</u>です。

(　　　　　)

A Practice writing the new *kanji*.

Write each *kanji* by first tracing each stroke in the correct order shown below. Complete all of the boxes by writing the entire *kanji* in the correct order in each box.

13	火 fire	か ひ び	かようび 火曜日 Tuesday ひ 火 fire	び はな火 fireworks

火 火 火 火
火 火 火

14	水 water	みず すい	みず お水 water	すいようび 水曜日 Wednesday

水 水 水 水
水 水 水

15	木 tree	き もく	き 木 tree	もくようび 木曜日 Thursday

木 木 木 木
木 木 木

16	金 gold	かね きん	かね お金 money	きんようび 金曜日 Friday

金 金 金 金 金 金 金
金 金 金

17	土 soil	ど つち	どようび 土曜日 Saturday				つち 土 soil				
			土	土	土						
			土	土	土						
18	本 book, origin	ほん もと ぽん ぼん	ほん 本 book にほん　にっぽん 日本 or 日本 Japan			やまもと 山本 Yamamoto (surname) さんぼん 三本 three (long, cylindrical objects)					
			本	本	本	本	本				
			本	本	本						
	Recognition Kanji Day of the week	曜	にちようび 日曜日 Sunday げつようび 月曜日 Monday								

B **Match each of the days of the week in the chart below with the letter of the corresponding illustration and the number of the corresponding *kanji* character.**

Example: Sunday	Monday	Tuesday	Wednesday	Thursday	Friday	Saturday
a						
1						

a.	b.	c.	d.	e.	f.	g.
1. 日	2. 水	3. 金	4. 月	5. 火	6. 土	7. 木

A Circle the correct readings of the underlined *kanji* for days of the week below. Then write the English meanings of the days of the week in the blanks that follow.

Ex. 火曜日 (にち　げつ　(か)　すい　もく　きん　ど)ようび _____Tuesday_____

1. 月曜日　(にち　げつ　か　すい　もく　きん　ど)ようび _____

2. 金曜日　(にち　げつ　か　すい　もく　きん　ど)ようび _____

3. 木曜日　(にち　げつ　か　すい　もく　きん　ど)ようび _____

4. 日曜日　(にち　げつ　か　すい　もく　きん　ど)ようび _____

5. 土曜日　(にち　げつ　か　すい　もく　きん　ど)ようび _____

6. 水曜日　(にち　げつ　か　すい　もく　きん　ど)ようび _____

B Study the pictures below, then circle the response in each corresponding sentence that correctly describes the picture.

1. お(火　水　木　金)を　のみます。

2. 日本の　お(火　水　金　土)では　ありません。

3. (火　水　木　本)を　よみます。

4. (火　水　木　本)は　日本語で　何と　いいますか。

5. 田中さんは　日(火　水　木　本)人です。

1.　　2.　　3.　　4.　　5.

C Study the calendar, then write the correct *kanji* in the ( ) to correctly complete each of the statements below.

Sun	Mon	Tue	Wed	Thu	Fri	Sat
1	2	3	4	5	6	7
8	9	10	11	12	13	14
15	16 敬老の日	17	18	19	20	21
22	23 秋分の日	24	25	26	27	28
29	30					

1. 1日は　（　　）曜日です。

2. 2日は　（　　）曜日です。

3. 3日は　（　　）曜日です。

4. 4日は　（　　）曜日です。

5. 5日は　（　　）曜日です。

6. 6日は　（　　）曜日です。

7. 7日は　（　　）曜日です。

8. 10日は　（　　）曜日です。

9. 16日は　（　　）曜日です。

10. 27日は　（　　）曜日です。

11. 八日は　（　　）曜日です。

12. 十四日は　（　　）曜日です。

13. 二十五日は　（　　）曜日です。

14. 十九日は　（　　）曜日です。

15. 二十六日は　（　　）曜日です。

D Write the correct *kanji* for the underlined *hiragana* in the boxes below. Write the correct readings of the underlined *kanji* in *hiragana* in the ( ).

1. 私は　お<u>みず</u>を　のみます。　　□

2. <u>ほん</u>を　よみます。　　□

3. <u>にほん</u>語を　べんきょうします。　　□□

4. 私の　<u>名前</u>は　けんです。　　（　　　　　）

5. 今日は　<u>金曜日</u>です。　　（　　　　　　　）

6. <u>明日</u>は　<u>土曜日</u>です。　　（　　　　）（　　　　　　　）

A **Practice writing the new *kanji*.**

Write each *kanji* by first tracing each stroke in the correct order shown below. Complete all of the boxes by writing the entire *kanji* in the correct order in each box.

19	口 mouth	くち ぐち こう	くち 口 mouth　　　　　　じんこう 人口 population みずぐち 水口さん Mr./Ms. Mizuguchi

口 口 口
口 口 口

| 20 | 目
eye | め
もく | め
目 eye　　　　　　もく
目ひょう objective, target, goal |

目 目 目 目 目
目 目 目

| 21 | 耳
ear | みみ | みみ
耳 ear |

耳 耳 耳 耳 耳 耳
耳 耳 耳

| 22 | 手
hand | て
しゅ | て
手 hand
にが手 weak in, not do well with　　か手 singer
*下手 unskillful　　*上手 skillful |

手 手 手 手
手 手 手

NOTE: Irregular pronunciations are marked with a **＊**.

23	父 father	ちち とう	ちち 父 (own) father					とう お父さん (someone else's) father			
			父	父	父	父				
			父	父	父					
24	母 mother	はは かあ	はは 母 (own) mother					かあ お母さん (someone else's) mother			
			母	母	母	母	母			
			母	母	母					
	Recognition Kanji over; under	上 下	じょうず 上手 skillful へた 下手 unskillful								

B Match each of the English words in the chart below with the letter of the corresponding illustration and the number of the corresponding *kanji* character.

Example: moon, month	mouth	ear	eye	hand	mother	above	below	father
b								
4								

a. b. c. d. e. f. g. h. i.

1. 目   2. 耳   3. 父   4. 月   5. 口   6. 手   7. 母   8. 下   9. 上

A Circle the correct readings of the *kanji*.

Ex. 日本 （(にほん)　なまえ　あした）

1. 耳 （くち　め　みみ　て　あし）

2. 手 （くち　め　みみ　て　あし）

3. 目 （くち　め　みみ　て　あし）

4. 口 （くち　め　みみ　て　あし）

5. 母 （ちち　はは　あに　あね）

6. 父 （ちち　はは　あに　あね）

7. お父さん （おにいさん　おねえさん　おとうさん　おかあさん）

8. お母さん （おにいさん　おねえさん　おとうさん　おかあさん）

9. 上手 （すき　きらい　じょうず　へた）

10. 下手 （すき　きらい　じょうず　へた）

B Study the pictures below, then circle the response in each sentence that matches the picture.

1. （口　目　耳　手）で　食べます。

2. （口　目　耳　手）で　見ます。

3. （口　目　耳　手）で　聞きます。

4. （口　目　耳　手）で　かきます。

5. （お父さん　お母さん）は　ゴルフ^{gorufu}が　（上手　下手）です。

1.	2.	3.	4.	5.

漢字　KANJI

C Write the correct *kanji* for parts of the body in the boxes.

D Write the correct *kanji* for the underlined *hiragana* in the boxes below. Write the correct readings of the underlined *kanji* in *hiragana* in the ( ).

1. <u>はは</u>の　<u>たんじょうび</u>は、　<u>さんがつ</u>　<u>じゅうろくにち</u>です。

　　□　　　　　□　　□□　　□□□

　　ははは　うたが　<u>上手</u>です。　<u>め</u>と　<u>くち</u>が　^{おお}大きいです。

　　□　　　　　（　　　）　　□　□

　　すこし　<u>にほん</u>^ご語を　はなします。

　　　　　　　　□□

2. <u>ちち</u>の　<u>たんじょうび</u>は、　<u>ろくがつ</u>　<u>ここのか</u>です。

　　□　　　　　□　　□□□　□

　　<u>ちち</u>は　<u>て</u>が　^{おお}大きいです。　ピアノが　<u>上手</u>では　ありません。

　　□　　□　　　　　　　　　　　　　　（　　　　　）

名前 ______________________

日づけ ______________ ______ 曜日

7かA
漢字 ワークシート

Ⓐ Practice writing the new *kanji*.

Write each *kanji* by first tracing each stroke in the correct order shown below. Complete all of the boxes by writing the entire *kanji* in the correct order in each box.

25	分 minute	わ ふん ぷん	分(わ)かりません I don't understand.　三分(ぷん) three minutes 二分(ふん) two minutes　八分(はっぷん) eight minutes 分 分 分 分 分 分 分
26	行 to go	い こう	行(い)きます go　りょ行(こう) travel 行 行 行 行 行 行 行 行 行
27	来 to come	き	来(き)ます come 来 来 来 来 来 来 来 来 来 来
28	車 car	くるま しゃ	車(くるま) car　でん車(しゃ) electric train じどう車(しゃ) car　じてん車(しゃ) bicycle 車 車 車 車 車 車 車 車 車 車

29	山 mountain	やま さん	やま 山 mountain ふ じ さん　ふ じ やま 富士山 or 富士山 Mt. Fuji やまもと 山本さん Mr./Ms. Yamamoto			やまぐち 山口さん Mr./Ms. Yamaguchi やまて 山手さん Mr./Ms. Yamate

			山	山	山				
			山	山	山				

30	川 river	かわ がわ	かわ 川 river かわもと 川本さん Mr./Ms. Kawamoto			かわぐち 川口さん Mr./Ms. Kawaguchi やまかわ 山川さん Mr./Ms. Yamakawa

			川	川	川				
			川	川	川				

Recognition Kanji o'clock	時	いちじ 一時 one o'clock

B Match each of the English words in the chart below with the letter of the corresponding illustration and the number of the corresponding *kanji* character.

mother	time, o'clock	minute	go	come	car	mountain	river
d							
8							

a.   b.   c.   d.   e.   f.   g.   h.

1. 川   2. 来   3. 車   4. 分   5. 山   6. 行   7. 時   8. 母

名前 _____

日づけ _____ _____ 曜日

A **Create your own story for each *kanji* in English.**

Ex. Why do "soil" and "measurement (one-tenth)" mean "temple"?

 "soil" + "measurement (one-tenth)" = 寺 "temple"

My story: At the temple, the monks measure plots of farm land to grow their crops. _____

1. Why do "sun" and "temple" mean "time, o'clock"?

(⊙) "sun" + 寺 "temple" = 時 "time, o'clock"

My story: _____

2. Why do "eight" and "sword" mean "minute"?

"eight" + "a sword" = 分 "minute"

My story: _____

3. Why do "grain" mean "to come"?

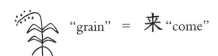 "grain" = 来 "come"

My story: _____

B **Circle the correct reading of each *kanji*.**

Ex. 川 (くるま　やま　(かわ))

1. 車 (くるま　やま　かわ)

2. 山 (くるま　やま　かわ)

3. 来ます (きます　いきます)

4. 行きます (きます　いきます)

5. 2分 に (ふん　ぷん)

6. 3分 さん (ふん　ぷん)

C Read the *kanji* and write each time in numeric form.

Ex. 九時十五分　（　9:15　）

1. 三時二十分　（　　　　　　）　　　3. 九時四十五分（　　　　　　）

2. 八時三十分　（　　　　　　）　　　4. 四時五十分（　　　　　　）

D Circle the correct *kanji* based on the context of the sentence.

1. 私(わたし)は　日曜日の　十(時　分)はんに　おきました。

2. 私(わたし)は　学校(がっこう)へ　（耳　車　目)で　行きます。

3. 「今(いま)、何(なん)(分　時)ですか。」「二(分　時)　五(分　時)です。」

4. （山　川)へ　（行　来)きましょう。　そして、スキー(sukii)を　しましょう。

E Write the correct *kanji* in the boxes below the underlined *hiragana*. Write the correct *hiragana* readings in the (　) below the underlined *kanji*.

1. ちちと　はは は　にほん語(ご)が　すこし　わかります。
　□　　□　　□　□　　　　　　　□

2. ともだちは　ど曜びに　くるまで　うちに　きました。
　　　　　　　□□　　□　　　　　□

3. 山本さんは　七時　じゅうごふんごろに　でんしゃで　学校(がっこう)へ　いきます。
　（　　　）（　　　）□□□　　　　　□　　　　　　　□

名前 _____

日づけ _____ _____ 曜日

A Practice writing the new *kanji*.

Write each *kanji* by first tracing each stroke in the correct order shown below. Complete all of the boxes by writing the entire *kanji* in the correct order in each box.

| 31 | 人 person | ひと にん じん | あの人 that person（ひと）
三人 three (people)（さんにん）
日本人 Japanese person（にほんじん） | *一人 one (person)（ひとり）
*二人 two (people)（ふたり） |

人 人
人 人 人

| 32 | 子 child | こ | 子ども child（こ） |

子 子 子
子 子 子

| 33 | 女 female | おんな | 女の人 woman, lady（おんな ひと） 女の子 girl（おんな こ） |

女 女 女
女 女 女

| 34 | 好 like | す(き) | 好き like（す） |

好 好 好 好 好 好
好 好 好

NOTE: Irregular readings are indicated by **∗**.

漢字 KANJI

| 35 | 田
rice
field | た
だ | たぐち
田口さん Mr./Ms. Taguchi　　　　かねだ
金田さん Mr./Ms. Kaneda
たがわ
田川さん Mr./Ms. Tagawa　　　やまだ
山田さん Mr./Ms. Yamada
ほんだ
本田さん Mr./Ms. Honda |

田 田 田 田 田

田 田 田

| 36 | 男
male | おとこ | おとこ ひと
男の人 man　　　　　おとこ こ こ
男の子 boy |

男 男 男 男 男 男 男

男 男 男

| **Recognition
Kanji
I** | 私 | わたし　　　やまだ
私は　山田です。 I am Yamada.
わたくし　　　やまだ
私 は　山田です。 I am Yamada. (formal) |

B Match each of the English words in the chart below with the letter of the corresponding illustration and the number of the corresponding *kanji* character.

mountain	person	child	female	man	rice field	I, me	like
a							
5							

a.   b.   c.   d.   e.   f.   g.   h.

1. 田　　2. 人　　3. 私　　4. 子　　5. 山　　6. 女　　7. 男　　8. 好

A **Create your own story for each *kanji* in English.**

Ex. Why do "harvest" and "mine" mean "I, me"?

"harvest" + "mine" = 私 "I, me"

My story: The harvested grain I am holding in my arm is mine. _____

1. Why do "rice field" and "power" mean "male"?

"rice field" + "power" = 男 "male"

My story: _____

2. Why do "female" and "child" mean "like"?

"female" + "child" = 好 "like"

My story: _____

B **Match each *kanji* with the letter of its correct reading from the box below.**

1. 人 ( )　　2. 子 ( )　　3. 女 ( )　　4. 好 ( )

5. 田 ( )　　6. 男 ( )　　7. 私 ( )

a. た　b. おとこ　c. こ　d. ひと　e. わたし　f. おんな　g. す(き)

C Circle the correct reading of the underlined *kanji* based on the context.

1. 日本<u>人</u>　（ ひと　にん　じん ）

2. 女の<u>人</u>　（ ひと　にん　じん ）

3. 三<u>人</u>　　（ ひと　にん　じん ）

4. <u>一人</u>　　（ ひとつ　ひとり　ふたり ）

5. <u>田</u>口さん　（ た　だ ）

6. 本<u>田</u>さん　（ た　だ ）

7. <u>川</u>本さん　（ かわ　がわ ）

8. 田<u>川</u>さん　（ かわ　がわ ）

D Circle the corresponding *kanji* for each name given in *hiragana*.

1. ほんださん　（ 金田さん　山田さん　本田さん ）

2. やまかわさん　（ 田口さん　田川さん　山川さん ）

3. みずぐちさん　（ 山手さん　山口さん　水口さん　木本さん ）

4. たぐちさん　（田川さん　金田さん　田口さん）

E Write the correct *kanji* in the boxes below the underlined *hiragana*.

1. <u>やまだ</u>さんは　<u>おんな</u>の　<u>こ</u>です。　そして、<u>くるま</u>が　<u>すき</u>です。

☐☐　　☐　　☐　　　　☐　　☐

2. あの　<u>おとこ</u>の　<u>ひと</u>は　<u>にほんじん</u>では　ありません。

☐　　☐　☐☐☐

名前 _____

日づけ _____ _____ 曜日

A Practice writing the new *kanji*.

Write each *kanji* by first tracing each stroke in the correct order shown below. Complete all of the boxes by writing the entire *kanji* in the correct order in each box.

37	先 first, previous	せん	せんせい 先生 teacher				せん 先しゅう last week			
			先	先	先	先	先	先		
			先	先	先					

38	生 be born, person	せい	せんせい 先生 teacher せいと 生徒 student (pre-college)			がくせい 学生 college student			
			生	生	生	生	生		
			生	生	生				

39	今 now	いま こん	いま　いちじ 今　一時です。It's now one. いまだ 今田さん　Mr./Ms. Imada こん 今しゅう this week		こんばん 今晩 tonight けさ *今朝 this morning きょう *今日 today		
			今	今	今	今	
			今	今	今		

40	毎 every	まい	まいにち 毎日 every day まいつき 毎月 every month		まいとし　まいねん 毎年　毎年 every year まい 毎しゅう every week			
			毎	毎	毎	毎	毎	毎
			毎	毎	毎			

NOTE: Irregular readings are indicated by ✳.

41	年 year	とし ねん	こ と し 今年 this year まい とし　　まい ねん 毎年 or 毎年 every year ねん きょ年 last year	らい ねん 来年 next year い ち ねん 一年 one year さん ねん せい 三年生 third grader
			年 年 年 年 年 年	
			年 年 年	
42	休 rest, absent	やす(み)	やす お休み holiday, day off	
			休 休 休 休 休 休	
			休 休 休	
	Recognition Kanji student	生徒	せい と 生徒 student (pre-college)	
	New Reading next	らい	らい ねん 来年 next year	らい げつ 来月 next month

B Match each of the English words in the chart below with the letter of the corresponding illustration and the number of the corresponding *kanji* character.

first, previous	be born, life	child	now	every	year	rest. absent	male
e							
5							

a.   b.   c.   d.   e.   f.   g.   h.

1. 今   2. 休   3. 毎   4. 子   5. 先   6. 年   7. 男   8. 生

Ⓐ Create your own story for each *kanji* in English.

Ex. Why do "to point," "ground" and "legs" mean "first, previous"?

 "point" + (土) "soil, ground" + "legs" = 先 "first, previous"

My story: First, the teacher points the way to go on the ground. _____

1. Why do "point" and "sprouts" mean "be born, life"?

"point" + "sprouts" = 生 "be born, person"

My story: _____

2. Why do "three people" and "go or come" mean "now"?

"three people" + "go or come" = 今 "now"

My story: _____

3. Why do "point," "one," and "mother" mean "every"?

"point" + 一 "one" + (母) "mother" = 毎 "every"

My story: _____

4. Why do "person" and "tree" mean "rest, vacation"?

(人) "person" + (木) "tree" = 休 "rest, vacation"

My story: _____

漢字

KANJI

B Match each *kanji* with the letter of its correct reading from the box.
Some *kanji* have two readings.

1. 今 ( )/( )　　2. 先 ( )　　3. 生 ( )

4. 年 ( )/( )　　5. 毎 ( )　　6. 休 ( ) み

| a. まい　b. ねん　c. やす　d. いま　e. こん　f. せん　g. とし　h. せい |

C Circle the correct reading of the underlined *kanji* based on the context.

1. 今しゅう（せん　こん　らい　まい）しゅう　　5. 今日 （あした　きょう）

2. 先しゅう（せん　こん　らい　まい）しゅう　　6. 今年 （ことし　きょねん）

3. 来しゅう（せん　こん　らい　まい）しゅう　　7. 今 　（いま　こん）

4. 毎日 　（せん　こん　らい　まい）にち　　8. 生徒 （がくせい　せいと）

D Write the correct *kanji* in the boxes below the underlined *hiragana*. Write the correct *hiragana*
readings in the ( ) below the underlined *kanji*.

1. せんせいは　今日も　おやすみです。

□□　（　　　）　□

2. 私は　　ことし　　さんねんせいです。

（　　）□□　□□□

A **Practice writing the new *kanji*.**

Write each *kanji* by first tracing each stroke in the correct order shown below. Complete all of the boxes by writing the entire *kanji* in the correct order in each box.

43	大 big	おお (きい) だい	おお 大きい　目 big eyes　　め だいす 大好き like very much	だいがくせい 大学生 college student おおやま 大山さん Mr./Ms. Oyama

大 大 大 □ □ □ □ □
大 大 大 □ □ □ □ □

44	小 small	ちい (さい) しょう	ちい 小さい small しょうがっこう 小学校 elementary school	しょうがくせい 小学生 elementary school student おがわ *小川さん Mr./Ms. Ogawa

小 小 小 □ □ □ □ □
小 小 小 □ □ □ □ □

45	中 inside, middle	なか ちゅう	なかもと 中本さん Mr./Ms. Nakamoto なかぐち 中口さん Mr./Ms. Nakaguchi	ちゅうがっこう 中学校 intermediate school ちゅうがくせい 中学生 int. school student

中 中 中 中 □ □ □ □
中 中 中 □ □ □ □ □

46	早 early (time)	はや (い)	はや 早い early	はやかわ 早川さん Mr./Ms. Hayakawa

早 早 早 早 早 早 □ □
早 早 早 □ □ □ □ □

NOTE: Irregular readings are indicated by **＊**.

漢字　KANJI

47	学 to study	がく がっ	がくせい 学生 college student だいがく 大学 college, university	ちゅうがくせい 中学生 int. school student がっこう 学校 school

学	学	学	学	学	学	学	学		
学	学	学							

48	校 school	こう	がっこう 学校 school しょうがっこう 小学校 elementary school	ちゅうがっこう 中学校 intermediate school こうこう 高校 high school

校	校	校	校	校	校	校	校	校	校
校	校	校							

Recognition Kanji high school	高校	こうこう 高校 high school

B Match each of the English words in the chart below with the letter of the corresponding illustration and the number of the corresponding *kanji* character.

	year	big	small	medium	early	study	school	be born, life
a								
2								

a.	b.	c.	d.	e.	f.	g.	h.

1. 大　2. 年　3. 学　4. 校　5. 早　6. 中　7. 生　8. 小

A **Create your own story for each *kanji* in English.**

Ex. Why do "school roof with the school emblem" and "child" mean "study"?

〔※〕 "school roof with the school emblem" + ☺ (子) "child" = 学 "study"

My story: Children study under the roof of the school, which displays the school emblem.

1. Why do "tree" and "six students sit with their legs crossed" mean "school"?

(木) "tree" + ☺ "six students sit with their legs crossed" = 校 "school"

My story: _____

2. Why do "sun, day" and "ten" mean "early"?

(日) "sun, day" + (十) "ten" = 早 "early"

My story: _____

B **Match each *kanji* with the letter of its correct reading from the box.**
Some *kanji* have two readings.

1. 大 (　　)/(　　)きい　　　3. 早 (　　)い　　　5. 校 (　　)

2. 小 (　　)/(　　)さい　　　4. 学 (　　)　　　6. 中 (　　)がく

| a. しょう　b. はや　c. だい　d. こう　e. おお　f. ちゅう　g. ちい　h. がく |

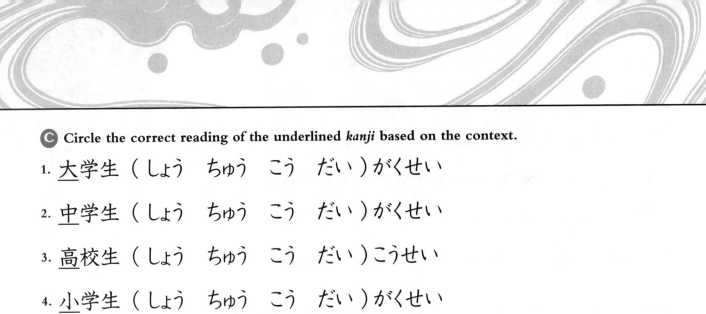

C Circle the correct reading of the underlined *kanji* based on the context.

1. 大学生 (しょう　ちゅう　こう　だい) がくせい

2. 中学生 (しょう　ちゅう　こう　だい) がくせい

3. 高校生 (しょう　ちゅう　こう　だい) こうせい

4. 小学生 (しょう　ちゅう　こう　だい) がくせい

5. 今月 (せん　こん　らい　まい) げつ

6. 先月 (せん　こん　らい　まい) げつ

7. 毎月 (せん　こん　らい　まい) つき

8. 来月 (せん　こん　らい　まい) げつ

D Write the correct *kanji* in the boxes below the underlined *hiragana*. Write the correct *hiragana* readings in the ( ) below the underlined *kanji*.

1. せんせいの　めは　おおきいですが、くちは　ちいさいです。
   □□　□　□　　　□　　□

2. 小川さんは　がっこうへ　七時に　いきます。　はやいですね。
   (　　　　) □□ (　　　) □　　□

3. ははは　いま　だいがくせいです。　がっこうが　だいすきです。
   □　□　□□□　　　□□　□□

A Practice writing the new *kanji*.

Write each *kanji* by first tracing each stroke in the correct order shown below. Complete all of the boxes by writing the entire *kanji* in the correct order in each box.

| 49 | 白 white | しろ | しろ
白い　くつ white shoes | | | | | |

白 白 白 白 白

白 白 白

| 50 | 百 hundred | ひゃく
びゃく
ぴゃく | ひゃく
百ドル one hundred dollars　　　　　　ろっぴゃく
六百ドル six hundred dollars
さんびゃく
三百ドル three hundred dollars　　　　　はっぴゃく
八百ドル eight hundred dollars |

百 百 百 百 百 百

百 百 百

| 51 | 千 thousand | せん
ぜん | せん
千 one thousand　　　　　　　さんぜん
三千 three thousand
はっせん
八千 eight thousand　　　　　　　なんぜん
何千 How many thousand? |

千 千 千

千 千 千

| 52 | 万 ten thousand | まん | いちまん
一万 10,000 (ten thousand)　　　　ひゃくまん
百万 1,000,000 (one million)
じゅうまん
十万 100,000 (hundred thousand) |

万 万 万

万 万 万

53	円 yen	えん	いちえん 一円 one yen じゅうえん 十円 ten yen	せんえん 千円 thousand yen いちまんえん 一万円 ten thousand yen

円	円	円	円						
円	円	円							

54	見 see, look, watch	み(る)	み 見せて ください。Please show me. み 見て ください。Please look.

見	見	見	見	見	見	見			
見	見	見							

Recognition Kanji dog	犬	おお　　　いぬ 大きい 犬 a big dog
Recognition Kanji fat, heavy	太 (る)	ふと 太って います is fat, heavy

B Match each of the English words in the chart below with the letter of the corresponding illustration and the number of the corresponding *kanji* character.

white	hundred	thousand	ten thousand	yen	look, see	dog	fat
b							
3							

a.　　b.　　c.　　d.　　e.　　f.　　g.　　h.

1. 犬　2. 見　3. 白　4. 千　5. 太　6. 万　7. 百　8. 円

A Create your own story for each *kanji* in English.

Ex. Why do "one" and "sun's rays" mean "one hundred"?

 "one" + "sun's rays" = 百 "one hundred"

My story: One white coin is a 100 yen. _____

1. Why do "cottage" and "window" mean "yen"?

⌂ "cottage" + ⊞ "window" = 円 "yen"

My story: _____

2. Why do "eye" and "legs" mean "look, see, watch"?

👁 "eye" + 儿 "legs" = 見 "look, see, watch"

My story: _____

B Match each *kanji* with the letter of its correct reading from the box.

1. 犬 (　　　)　　3. 白 (　　　)　　5. 千 (　　　)　　7. 円 (　　　)

2. 太 (　　　)　　4. 百 (　　　)　　6. 万 (　　　)　　8. 見 (　　　)

| a. ひゃく b. まん c. いぬ d. えん e. しろ f. せん g. み(る) h. ふと(る) |

C Match each underlined *kanji* with its correct reading from the box based on the context.

1. 五<u>千</u> (　　　)　　3. 三<u>千</u> (　　　)　　5. 四<u>万</u> (　　　)

2. 七<u>百</u> (　　　)　　4. 三<u>百</u> (　　　)　　6. 六<u>百</u> (　　　)

| a. ひゃく b. びゃく c. ぴゃく d. せん e. ぜん f. まん |

漢字 KANJI

D Write the prices written below in *kanji* in numeric form with the yen symbol.

Ex. 五千二百円　（　¥5,200　）

1. 一万七千円　（　　　　　　）

2. 八百四十九円　（　　　　　　）

3. 六万五千三十円　（　　　　　　）

E Write the correct *kanji* in the boxes below the underlined *hiragana*. Write the correct *hiragana* readings in the ( ) below the underlined *kanji*.

1. しろい　犬は　にまんさんぜんごひゃくえんです。

　□　（　）□□□□□□□

2. 私の　ちちも　ははも　ちょっと　太って　います。

　　□□　　　　　（　　　）

3. せんせい、　この　にほんの　お金を　みて　ください。

　□□　　　□□（　　）□

A **Practice writing the new *kanji*.**

Write each *kanji* by first tracing each stroke in the correct order shown below. Complete all of the boxes by writing the entire *kanji* in the correct order in each box.

55	天 heaven	てん	お天き weather　　天ぷら tempura 天 天 天 天 天 天 天
56	牛 cow	うし ぎゅう	牛 うし 牛乳 (cow's) milk 牛 牛 牛 牛 牛 牛 牛
57	良 good	よ(い)	良くないです is not good 良 良 良 良 良 良 良 良 良 良
58	食 to eat	た(べる) しょく	食べます eat 食事を します dine, have a meal 食 食 食 食 食 食 食 食 食 食 食 食

59	言 to say	い(う)	言って ください。 Please say it. 何と 言いますか。 What is it called?

言 言 言 言 言 言 言
言 言 言

60	語 language	ご	日本語 Japanese language　　　えい語 English language

語 語 語 語 語 語 語 語
語 語 語

New Reading one (cup)	いっ	一杯の　コーヒー one cup of coffee	
Recognition Kanji What?	何	何人 What nationality? 何語 What language?	何日 What day of the month? 何人 How many people?

B Match each of the English words in the chart below with the letter of the corresponding illustration and the number of the corresponding *kanji* character.

water	heaven	cow	good	eat	say	language	what
b							
4							

a. **b.** **c.** **d.** **e.** **f.** **g.** **h.**

1. 言　2. 牛　3. 何　4. 水　5. 良　6. 天　7. 語　8. 食

A Create your own story for each *kanji* in English.

Ex. Why do "sky" and "big" mean "heaven"?

 "sky" + ⚡ "big" = 天 "heaven"

My story: <u>The Big Man in the sky waits in heaven.</u>

1. Why do "roof" and "good" mean "eat"?

"roof" + "good" = 食 "eat"

My story: _____

2. Why do "say" and "five + mouth" mean "language"?

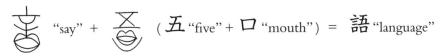 "say" + (五 "five" + 口 "mouth") = 語 "language"

My story: _____

B Match each *kanji* with the letter of its correct reading from the box.

1. <u>良</u>い （　　） 　 4. <u>言</u>います （　　） 　 7. 何<u>語</u> （　　　）

2. <u>何</u>語 （　　） 　 5. <u>食</u>べます （　　） 　 8. <u>食</u>じを　します （　　）

3. <u>何</u>日 （　　） 　 6. <u>生</u>にゅう （　　） 　 9. <u>天</u>ぷら （　　）

| a. い b. ご c. た d. よ e. なに f. なん g. てん h. しょく i. ぎゅう |

漢字

KANJI

C Match each *kanji* with the letter of its correct reading from the box based on the context.

| a. いち b. ひと c. いっ d. に e. ふた f. ろっ g. さん h. みっ i. はっ |

1. 一つ　　（　　　）　　5. 一ぱい　　（　　　　　）

2. 二つ　　（　　　）　　6. 二はい　　（　　　　　）

3. 三つ　　（　　　）　　7. 三人　　（　　　　　）

4. 六ぱい　（　　　）　　8. 八ぱい　　（　　　　　）

D Write the correct *kanji* in the boxes below the underlined *hiragana*. Write the correct *hiragana* readings in the (　) below the underlined *kanji*.

1. きょう　おてんきは　よくなかったです。

☐☐☐　　☐

2. 私は　まいにち　あさ　ぎゅうにゅうを　のんで、パンを　たべます。

☐☐　　☐　　　　　　☐

3. せんせい、　tree は　にほんごで　何と　いいますか。

☐☐　　☐☐☐（　　）☐

4. ははは　てんぷらが　だいすきです。

☐　　☐　　☐☐

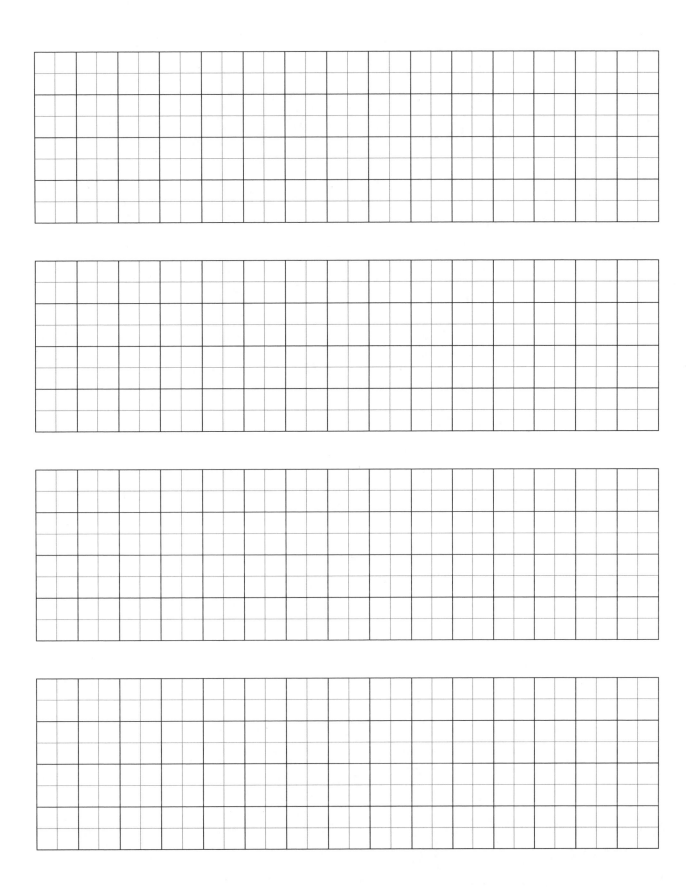

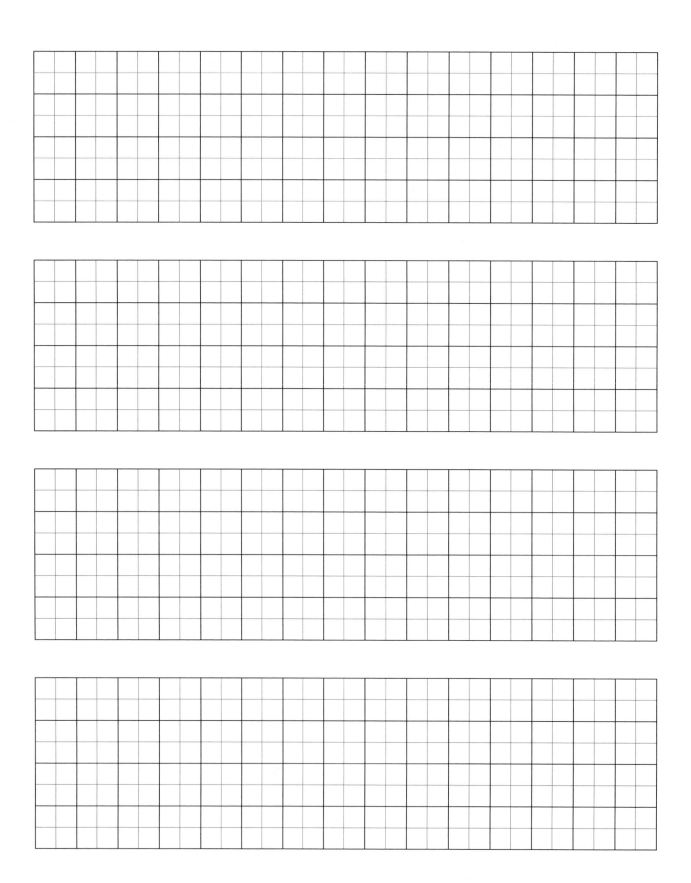

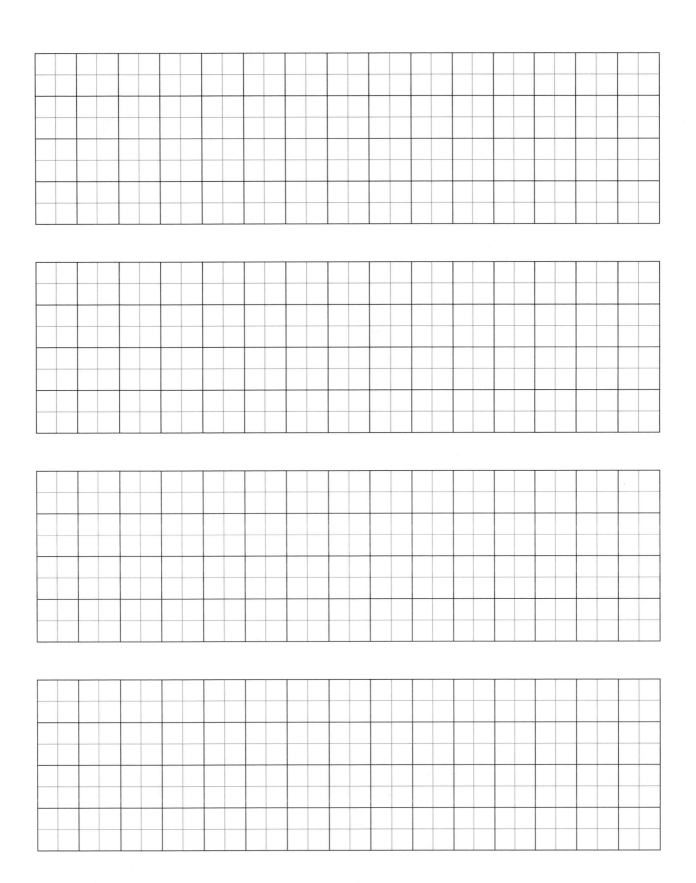

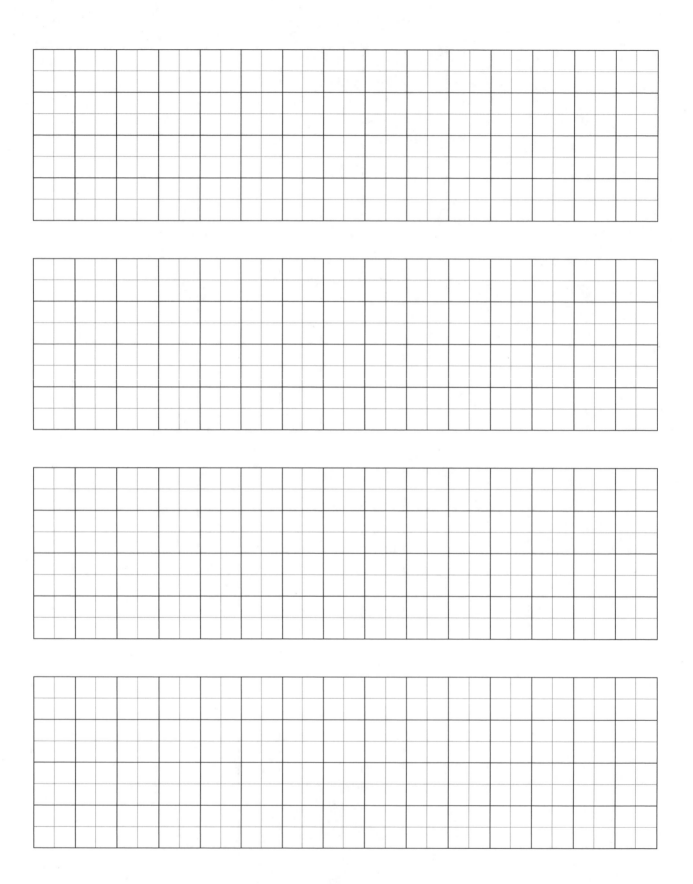